Yoga Chakra

With kind regards, ॐ and prem

Swami Niranjan

Yoga Chakra

The Wheel of Yoga

Swami Niranjanananda Saraswati

Yoga Publications Trust, Munger, Bihar, India

Printed by Yoga Publications Trust
    First edition 2014

ISBN: 978-93-84753-20-7

Publisher and distributor: Yoga Publications Trust, Ganga Darshan, Munger, Bihar, India.

Website: www.biharyoga.net

Printed at Aegean Offset Printers, Greater Noida

Dedication

*In humility we offer this dedication to
Swami Sivananda Saraswati, who initiated
Swami Satyananda Saraswati into the secrets of yoga.*

Contents

Such is of the course of deeds that move the wheels of the world: small hands do them because they must, while the eyes of the great are elsewhere.

—J.R.R. Tolkien, *Lord of the Rings*

In August 2014 Swami Niranjan gave a series of lectures to the Yoga Instructor Course students, sannyasins, sannyasa trainees and students of the One-year Diploma in Yogic Studies at Ganga Darshan in which he explained the origin, evolution and expansion of yoga. He shared the unique history of the Satyananda Yoga–Bihar Yoga Tradition, and described the role the new teachers and sannyasins would be taking in the development of its future.

1

First Waves of Yoga

When you hear the word yoga, you conjure up an image in your mind of what yoga is for you. Some people think of a fakir sitting on a bed of nails, meditating, and they believe that is yoga. Some people conjure up the image of a yogi sitting in a cave in the mountains, and they associate that with yoga. Some people see a pictorial representation of kundalini moving up the spine, and they become interested in yoga. Other people go to a yoga studio and do yoga aerobics in front of full-length mirrors. They watch their bodies, observe their posture and believe yoga to be something physical that brings the body into a nice shape.

Each person conjures up an idea or an image about yoga and that is how the identification with yoga begins. There are many ideas, thoughts and images that you create in your mind which define what yoga is for you; however, yoga is not any of these ideas. What then is yoga?

In the ancient times, yoga was seen as a form of personal discipline. Different people from various ages, who today are known as masters or sages, developed a branch of yoga. About five thousand years ago, Patanjali perfected an aspect of yoga – the mental aspect of yoga – and wrote a thesis on the subject, the *Yoga Sutras*.

Credit goes to Patanjali for writing the dissertation on raja yoga, and credit goes to Swatmarama and Gheranda for writing the dissertations on hatha yoga. Credit goes to

Shandilya and Narada for writing their theses on bhakti yoga. They all maintained, however, that their work was a continuation from a prior thought to the next thought. No yoga was ever seen as complete in itself; rather, each aspect of yoga complemented the other. Thus, in the ancient times the sages linked their teachings, created a sequence, and developed these systems of yoga.

Yoga as a subject, though, predates the time period of these masters. Patanjali is not the founder or creator of yoga, and neither is anyone else from the ancient period who wrote on yoga, since the subject of yoga existed long before them. These people simply did their doctorate theses on different subjects of yoga, which predated them by many millennia. References to yoga are found in scriptures and in histories that predate even Krishna and Rama and go into an earlier age, that of Satya Yuga.

Salutations to the original yogi

Who started yoga if not these people? The answer is given in tantra, which states that Shiva is the first propagator of yoga, and while he was describing yoga to his disciple, Parvati, other beings heard the teachings. These beings

became the medium to bring the yogic teachings of Shiva to earth. Before Patanjali, Swatmarama and Gheranda, there was an existing tradition of masters starting with Shiva, who brought the teachings of yoga to human society. Exactly when that was, we do not know. What we do know is that yoga existed in many of the ancient cultures and civilizations of the world.

Parvati and Shiva

Preservation of a universal culture

In the 1970s I undertook research on the pre-Colum-bian cultures of Central and South America: the Aztecs, the Incas, the Chibchas and the Mayans. Through research I discovered a lot of yoga-related evidence. In their sacred book, which is known as *Popol Vuh*, you find references to yoga asanas, yoga pranayamas and the chakras. You see the images and the symbols: the triangle,

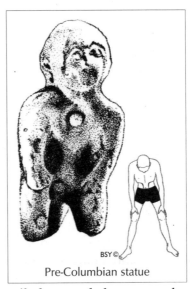

Pre-Columbian statue

the Shivalingam, the serpent coiled around the stone, the serpent ascending the spine. There are the practices of shatkarmas: trataka, nauli, the practice of kunjal. There are the postures: shoulder stand, scorpion pose, headstand, thunderbolt pose.

One finds so many yoga references, to asana, pranayama, mudra, bandha, and meditation; and not only literal references, but also statues now found in the preserves and museums which have been carbon-dated to 2,000 and 3,000 BC. These statues depict perfect yoga postures. Similar findings were made in the old cultures of the Scandinavian countries and in the old cultures of Africa. From all this evidence, it seems that once upon a time yoga was a global practice, system and culture. It was not confined only to India.

It is speculated that due to geological changes, climatic changes, tribal wars, invasions and migrations, many of these practices were lost; however, they were preserved by the Asian nations, which have retained remnants of the yogic tradition in their cultures even today. After a gap of many years the present revival of yoga took place from India, and therefore today yoga is seen as coming from India.

In India, yoga was protected by and associated with a specific group of people: the renunciates, the recluses, the sannyasins. The sannyasins preserved the knowledge and the tradition, and so yoga became tagged with them and people believed that they used yoga for enlightenment, for self-realization, and for awakening the dormant faculties.

It was from this point onwards that the global society began to conjure up an image of yoga in their minds. More specifically when the British came to India and encountered yoga, they saw people like me in one dhoti and said, "Oh, a fakir . . . " The association of yoga with 'fakirism' is a prominent idea today in the West due to the influence of the British notion that yoga is for renunciates and sannyasins seeking salvation, and is a part of the Indian religion, culture and belief system. As the British were the rulers, their mandates, writings and books were widely read and everybody held that opinion, although the British had no exposure to the culture and the traditions of India.

Yoga's three age imprints: early, middle, present

Yoga can be divided into three, distinct periods. The early period was the period of Shiva, Dattatreya, Vasishtha, Vishwamitra, Matsyendranath and Gorakhnath. The Nath

sampradaya, tradition or sect, came out of this early period. They were the early propagators of hatha yoga, raja yoga, kriya yoga and kundalini yoga. Although they were the propagators of all yogas, they focused more on physical discipline, on hatha yoga. That is the 'early period'.

The 'middle period' is the period of Patanjali, Gheranda, Swatmarama, and so on, who are the points of reference

Yogi Goraknath

4

for today's myriad of yoga practices. The middle period of Patanjali, Swatmarama and Gheranda has also delivered their classical texts and books, which we refer to today.

The late period is the present age, the last hundred years, when yoga re-emerged. These are the three age imprints in the life of yoga. The three time-stamps on yoga are: the early period, Shiva's time; the middle period, the time of Patanjali and others; the present period, the last hundred years of the re-emergence.

EARLY PERIOD OF YOGA

What was the aim of yoga in the early period? Shiva begins his teaching of yoga when Parvati asks him the question, "There is a lot of suffering in the world. How can it be ended?" Tantra and yoga emerged at Shiva's time to help alleviate suffering. That was the purpose of yoga; and the thought of Shiva in the exposition of yoga was clearly defined.

Shiva teaches Parvati

How was suffering defined in this early period? If you look at the scriptures, the sufferings defined in the early age are more mental and psychic, and less physical. Shiva said there are three kinds of suffering in the world: adhyatmika, adhibhautika, adhidaivika.

Adhidaivika means the suffering that is destined. You experience your life between birth and death, not beyond or before. Your understanding of life is only after you have taken birth until the point when you die, and you have no understanding of what happens before or what happens after. This journey from birth to death is known

5

as life, and this body, this entire creation, is made up of the combination and permutation of the five elements. Sentient and insentient life both exist due to the five elements.

These five elements are conditioned. They have their own nature, limitations and areas of function, and when they come together they come with these traits, which become destined. When the five tattwas become imbalanced they lead to disease. Many times you are unable to manage your sicknesses. They are not due to your imbalances in life, your routine or lifestyle, rather, are due to genetics; they are inherited. From where did you inherit these sicknesses? You say from your forefathers. Then from where did your forefathers inherit them? From imbalanced tattwas. These imbalanced tattwas exist in you in the form of a gene, and that is a cause of suffering. Thus, destiny is a cause of suffering. Karma is another cause of suffering. Those causes of suffering that cannot be controlled are known as adhidaivika or destined suffering.

Another type of suffering is known as *adhibhautika*, the suffering that comes from your environment and from your society. Natural calamities give birth to plagues and other factors that create suffering, both personal and social. That is the second kind of suffering.

The third kind of suffering is self-generated and is known as *adhyatmika*: individual stress and tension; the mind and the emotions; the expectations, desires, passions, greed, envy, jealousy, ego.

Therefore, yoga at the time of Shiva was a means to overcome these chronic imbalances and sufferings that restrict the creative expression of human life. At Shiva's time the aim of yoga was not self-realization, it was overcoming human suffering.

MIDDLE PERIOD OF YOGA

Next comes the middle period, which is the time of Patanjali, Gheranda and Swatmarama. They did their dissertations on what you know as hatha yoga and raja yoga. The names of the yogas that you know today have been given by this middle group of sages. The name of the original yoga was Pashupata yoga. That was the first and original yoga by Shiva. Pashupata yoga comprised of five sub-yogas: mantra yoga, sparsha yoga, bhava yoga, abhava yoga, and maha yoga. These were the original yogas that later on were further compartmentalized and given different names by this second group of masters: raja yoga, karma yoga, bhakti yoga, jnana yoga, hatha yoga, kriya yoga, kundalini yoga.

Creating balance with hatha yoga

In this middle period, the focus of yoga was balancing the pranic and the mental behaviour. That is how hatha yoga is defined by Swatmarama and Gheranda. Hatha yoga is a system to balance the forces of *ida* and *pingala*, the lunar and the solar forces; the sympathetic and parasympathetic forces. The present hatha yoga system is of Gheranda and Swatmarama, which has dynamic asanas, prana-yamas, mudras, bandhas and shatkarmas. These five aspects constitute hatha yoga. Hatha yoga is not only asana; asana is only one-fifth of hatha yoga, while four-fifths of hatha yoga is pranayama, mudra, bandha, and shatkarma. The purpose of hatha yoga is to realign the energy system, as it is believed that imbalance in these two energies creates illness in the body and in the mind.

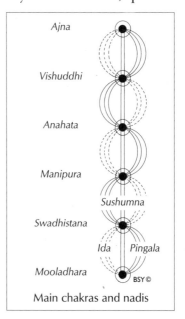

Main chakras and nadis

They also set the founda-tion for yoga therapy. Gheranda defines disease as the 'absence of ease from the body'. When the ease, comfort and harmony

7

of the body are gone or disturbed, then that state or condition is known as dis-ease, disturbed ease: disease. In the classical literature on hatha yoga you will read statements like, 'This asana is beneficial for removal of this ailment. This asana is beneficial for managing this disease. This asana is useful in curing this illness.' The sages are clear and specific about it. These yogis experimented and discovered that by managing the flow of ida and pingala through hatha yoga practices, you can overcome different kinds of physical and psychological ailments and diseases. The asanas have a particular effect on the body and help to eradicate illness and disease by realigning the ida and pingala forces. This is how the first concept of yoga therapy emerged.

Patanjali's exposition on yoga
Then the next progression was made into raja yoga, into Patanjali's system. After you have worked through your body, work through your mind. What is the focus of Patanjali's system of mind management? He does not say that in order to manage your mind you must attain samadhi, practise pranayama or practise asana. He says that in order to manage your mind, be a witness to the mind. His statement is, "To manage the mind, observe the mind." He emphasizes the aspect of *drashta*: observation, awareness and alertness to what is happening, what is transpiring inside the head. He emphasizes the management of *vrittis*, the modifications of mind, and says that yoga is managing the different vrittis. That is his emphasis, not samadhi, like many writers believe and state.

The yoga of Patanjali does not end in samadhi; samadhi is only one stage of yoga. It is an experience of yoga, just as asana is one experience of yoga. Pranayama is one experience of yoga. Ajapa japa is one experience of yoga. Yoga nidra is another experience of yoga, and in the same manner, samadhi is an experience of yoga. It is not the finality of yoga. For Patanjali, yoga is a discipline and this idea is summarized in the first three statements of the *Yoga Sutras*. Disciples ask him, "What is yoga?"

8

Patanjali says, "Yoga is a form of discipline." Sutra number one: *Atha yoga anushasanam*.

"What will happen with this discipline?"

"You will get control over the fluctuations of your mind." Sutra number two: *Yogah chitta vritti nirodhah*.

"What will happen when you have control over the mind?"

"When you have managed the upheavals of the mind you shall become the observer and realize your true nature; the peaceful, harmonious and joyous nature" – *Tadaa drashtuh svaroope avasthanam*. The third sutra.

Patanjali defines his understanding of yoga in these first three sutras, and the rest of the sutras are then the practices to help you to observe yourself. Patanjali says yama and niyama first. His emphasis does not begin with physical postures or breathing practices; his emphasis begins with behaviour. Start to observe and modify your behaviour. Learn to restrain your senses and mind from creating disturbances and wreaking havoc in your life. For this, yama and niyama have to be practised.

While you are managing the behaviours, the characteristics and habits of your mind, you also organize your body by becoming fixed, stable, and comfortable in any posture that you are in; that is the asana of Patanjali. In the *Yoga Sutras*, asana is defined as a posture in which you can remain steady and comfortable for an extended period of time without movement.

When you are sitting quietly and comfortably, that is Patanjali's asana. If you sit in a chair or on the floor without fidgeting, comfortable and still, for half an hour, twenty minutes, fifteen minutes or even ten minutes without moving, that is asana. If you are in headstand and you stay there for five minutes or ten minutes, that is asana. If you are in *mayurasana*,

Mayurasana

9

peacock pose, stay there, be comfortable and steady in that posture for half an hour, that is asana.

Sri Swamiji made us understand this when he taught us in the early sixties. He used to make us do asanas in sequence, and we had to stay in one pose till he corrected each person's posture. From the time he started going around making the corrections till the time he finished it would be half an hour, and we had to stay in the asana; and we did it! We were young, we were inspired and we liked the challenge, therefore we did it. That is how Sri Swamiji's first disciples realized that even if you are standing on one little finger, if you can be comfortable and still for ten minutes, you can meditate. That is the asana of Patanjali. Patanjali's focus was not on exercise. His focus was on stillness, to stimulate mental stability and concentration.

It is the same principle with pranayama. Patanjali says that inhalation is one type of pranayama; exhalation is the second type of pranayama; and holding the breath is the third type of pranayama. According to him, the normal breath is pranayama and you do not have to breathe through your nostrils alternately or go through all the heavy breathing exercises.

From behaviour and character management he immediately shifts to stability of body, brain and mind, then to pratyahara, dharana, dhyana and samadhi. Out of the eight stages of Patanjali's yoga, six are purely attitudinal and mental, and only two are aids to give you stability, firmness and concentration. Patanjali was not a hatha yoga teacher but predominantly a meditation teacher.

Shandiliya's bhakti yoga
Shandiliya defines bhakti yoga as a means to manage one's emotions, not as devotion, rather as a scientific method of balancing the emotions. The word *bhakti* means devotion, but not bhakti yoga; they are two different things. As bhakti is devotion, people confuse bhakti yoga to be the yoga of devotion. It is not the yoga of devotion, it is the yoga of

emotion. Just as raja yoga is the yoga of mind, bhakti yoga is the yoga of emotion.

There are nine stages of bhakti yoga, just as in raja yoga there are eight stages and in hatha yoga there are five stages. Going through each of bhakti yoga's nine stages allows you to observe your emotional behaviours and expressions, and then harmonize, channel, transcend, transform and sublimate them.

In the middle age, yoga developed as a means to manage the imbalances of the body, which are rooted first in overcoming physical suffering, and then developing the creative faculties of mind and harmonizing the emotions.

Inner and outer yoga

Yoga was further divided into two different categories during this middle period, antaranga yoga and bahiranga yoga.

Antaranga means internal, and *antaranga yoga* is the internal yoga. It is the internal aspect of yoga which allows you to observe and change yourself. By practising these yogas you change your conditions, your environment, your mentality and your habits. You change your situation, and find your expression of creativity and the aim of life. Hatha yoga, raja yoga, kriya yoga and kundalini yoga are all part of antaranga yoga, the internal effort of yoga which has to be practised and perfected.

Bahiranga yoga is the yoga that is expressed; *bahiranga* means outer, expressive. Once you have perfected the inner yogas, then your social living needs to be guided by yogic principles, and that is where the expressive, external yogas become valuable. Karma yoga, jnana yoga and bhakti yoga are bahiranga yogas which you express.

CONCLUSION

In the early and middle periods of yoga, self-realization was not the aim of yoga. Rather, the aim of yoga was betterment of life and a qualitative attainment in life. Nowhere is the word 'realization' mentioned.

11

2

Contemporary Age: Yoga Goes Viral

The early period of yoga was dominated by the teachings of Lord Shiva. In the early period, the propagators of yoga were either people who had heard the teachings of yoga directly, or who were later considered to be incarnations of Shiva. They were followers of Pashupata yoga, the original yoga propounded by Shiva.

Pashu means animal; *pati* means master, therefore *pashupati* means master of animals or controller of animals. Thus Pashupata yoga is the yoga that leads to mastery over the lower, demonical, animalistic, tamasic tendencies of life and establishes one in the state of purity, *sattwa*. That is the definition of the word Pashupati: one who has attained mastery over animals. The vrittis and individual tendencies are seen as uncontrolled and wild animals, each one having its own separate, tamasic, limiting characteristic.

Pashupata yoga in its original form comprised of five different sub-yogas. The first was mantra yoga, and it appears that in the middle period concepts of mantra yoga and raja yoga evolved from the original mantra yoga of the Pashupata system. The second sub-yoga of the Pashupata system was sparsha yoga, which led to the development of hatha yoga and kundalini yoga in the middle period. The third was bhava yoga, which became bhakti yoga in the middle period. The fourth was abhava yoga, which became jnana yoga, establishment in the higher truth as a form of higher realization, higher identification and absorption in that state. The fifth was maha yoga, the expressive yoga which put together all the four aspects into creative expression. This was Pashupata yoga, comprised of five aspects, prevalent during Shiva's period.

Then there was a gap of time while people practised and perfected the Pashupata yoga. A renaissance took place in the middle age period. The advancements of these sadhanas were written down as experiences, realizations and observations of the seers' understanding, representing the upanishadic time when disciples would go to a *gurukul*, place of the guru, to learn and acquire knowledge. In the collection of the Upanishads, there are twenty-two that deal specifically with the subject of yoga. They talk of kundalini, chakras, pranayama, mudra, bandha, asana, yama and niyama. According to these texts there are many yamas and niyamas. There are over thirty-six yamas and thirty-six niyamas defined by the sages to their disciples in the Yoga Upanishads.

In the middle period of yoga a tradition developed of spiritual aspirants, spiritual discoverers and spiritual travellers. Out of this group emerged Patanjali, Gheranda, Swatmarama and other yogis including Shandilya and Narada, who each wrote a thesis on a specific aspect of yoga. This became the trend. Thus, the original yoga of Shiva's time was further elaborated upon by the sages, seers and aspirants of the middle period, and that is how the practice of yoga has been retained till today.

Contemporary yoga pioneers arise

The emergence of yoga in the present age, the third timeline of yoga, begins in the nineteenth century and continues into the twentieth and twenty-first centuries. Initially, this was the period when the British came to India and gradually started to rule the country. During their governance they came across a group of people who were different from the normal social groups; they wore a dhoti and an angavastra,

14

had shaved heads or long, matted hair; there were some with just a loincloth on the body, or they were people like us who were alien to the British mentality, ideology, culture, society and civilization. We the sannyasins and sadhus were labelled by the British as 'the fakirs', and India was perceived as the land of fakirs, all engaged in practising physical contortions: one leg tied here, one arm there, standing on one leg or doing something else that appeared unusual to these people. That was the image of the yogic and the sannyasin tradition which became commonly known in the West, as the British had control of information and technology.

Out of this group of fakirs emerged some who were able to integrate and talk about the tradition in a language that the outsiders could understand. One of the first to emerge in this manner was Yogi Ram Charaka in the nineteenth century. He was a sannyasin and a yogi, who wrote four books on raja yoga, karma yoga, hatha yoga, and jnana yoga, published in the late nineteenth century. The books were only about eighty or ninety pages long, yet they brought the first idea of yoga into the western culture. Yogi Ram Charaks teaching was in the form of philosophy and theory, not in the form of practices. Then, following the trend, Swami Vivekananda spoke on these four aspects of yoga.

During this period, a tradition of competent spiritual aspirants emerged who were associated with a remote Himalayan yogi called Babaji. These people became the advocates of Babaji's teachings: Sri Yukteshwar, Lahiri Mahashaya and Paramahamsa Yogananda. Around this same period came Ramana Maharshi and Anandamayi Ma. Ramana Maharshi followed the path of jnana yoga and Anandamayi Ma followed the path of bhakti yoga. The original information about yoga was confined to the theories of hatha yoga, raja yoga, karma yoga, jnana yoga, and the teachings of kriya yoga, which first emerged due to Paramahamsa Yogananda in the lineage of Babaji.

Around the 1920s and 1930s, another tradition evolved from the South, from the kingdom of Mysore, where yogasana was taught to the army men, using different types of props. That tradition was revived by Krishnamacharya and was carried forward by Desikachar and Mr Iyengar. They became the hatha yoga trainers, and they used the props that were used in the army of the Mysore kingdom for  stretching the body and for coming into specific postures.

At the same time, in the late 1920s, Swami Sivananda went to Rishikesh and started to explore the other forms of classical yogas. In the course of time he established his institution, the Divine Life Society, and in the thirties and forties he started training his disciples in yoga. After training his disciples he told them to go out into the country, into the world, and disseminate yoga.

In the fifties and sixties, the disciples of Swami Sivananda travelled. Swami Satchidananda, the founder of Integral Yoga Institute in the US, was sent to Colombo, Sri Lanka, and from there to New York. He started teaching hatha yoga and raja yoga as an integral yoga system. Swami Vishnudevananda was sent to Germany, and after spending years in Germany he went to New York and then to Canada, where he established his centre and became a strong propagator of hatha yoga. Similarly, Swami Venkatesananda went to Australia, New Zealand and Mauritius, and became an exponent of raja yoga. Swami Sahajananda went to South Africa and started teaching hatha yoga and bhakti yoga. In this manner, the different disciples of Swami Sivananda took yoga wherever they went, according to their understanding and sadhana. The theory Swami Sivananda gave them was that yoga should integrate the faculties of head, heart and hands, and that became their focus.

Impact of information technology on human nature

In the age of Shiva, in the early timeline, yoga was used to manage and deal with self-generated, environmental, and destined suffering. In the second period, the middle period, yoga developed as a way to integrate human nature and the personality, and lead one to a deeper and higher realization of one's own potential. Yoga during this period was a means to develop the creative skills and abilities of the psyche, emotions and mind, leading to an enhanced or enlightened level of existence. This same idea was carried forward in the present day and age by Swami Sivananda, though in a more practical form. Today, people need to awaken and integrate the faculties of the head, the heart, and the hands, and these faculties can only be awakened if there is a true inclination and yearning to open oneself. Until this happens all yoga remains merely intellectual understanding or knowledge; it does not become experience.

We must look at our society, at the present time and age, and the upbringing of the new generation. The youth in their twenties are gradually coming into the mainstream of life. What in their background helps them to find their niche and their comfort zone in life? Does technology aid human development and growth, or does it hamper and restrict human creativity?

I travel to different places, and when I go to the beach to see the water and the sunset, I see the youth sitting there, looking at their mobiles and sending Facebook messages. Hardly anybody is looking at the beach or the sunset. Sometimes they say, "Swamiji, come, let us go to see the town at night." Six or eight people cram into a car, and I am the only one looking out the window, while the others are busy with their mobiles. We go to a restaurant, I am waiting for food, and the others are sending messages to their friends and writing on Facebook. There is no real communication.

These are bright young people with a lot of potential, energy and intelligence, however, the personal culture

Swami Sivananda and his disciples practising nauli

in their life is such that they are not sincere, they are not serious, they are not committed. When such people come to sannyasa, they reflect the absence of these three qualities.

Fractured mentality of hidden files

Observe the current situation of computer operators in the world, and the companies and industries in the world where computers are being used. I have asked people some questions: What do you do in your industry? What happens in your industry? What happens in your office? What happens in your area? They say, "Swamiji, there has been a seesaw change in the last two, three, four years, in people who come to our offices now, and we have had to cut all social media feedback from our offices. No computer has YouTube, Facebook or Gmail. Today everybody expects that when they go to an office they will use the office for their personal work and not for the official work." That is the tendency today.

18

On the screen they will have something official, yet privately they are doing something else, hiding it in folders and keeping it secret. This indicates the state of mind and disloyalty within each individual. That is how each one builds up their own hidden agendas in life. This is a behaviour trait; it is a character trait. There is no loyalty, understanding, connection, or feeling. Every-
thing is manipulation. On the surface, the screen shows the work is being done, yet secretly, different things are being downloaded. Different situations are being enacted, which all ride piggyback on the organization.

This indicates people's mentality and mindset today. Even in your personal life, all of you, in one way or the other, have many hidden folders which only you can access. When there were no computers, you had to hide it in your mind; then it was called suppression. When you hide it under layers of other things within your mind, this is called 'suppression', and it was once identified as a mental illness. You need to remove the blockages and to open up. As long as there is one hidden file, there will always be a problem in life.

On the one hand, your desired and expected inclination is to attain spiritual awareness, yet on the other hand the natural inclination is to hold on to what makes you an individual, unable to let go: 'I can't give my password, I can't give my this. I can't give my that!' When you hold on to these hidden folders that represent 'you', your individuality, where is your sincerity, commitment and seriousness? Your intentions contradict your actions, which is hypocrisy. Even the brightest people fall into the trap of their ambitions, and that limits their progress and growth in life.

This is where integrating the faculties of head, heart and hands plays a major role. You must integrate them with seriousness, sincerity, and commitment – and with loyalty. Otherwise what connection is there? Even for a sannyasin there is no connection with a guru if there is no loyalty. Today such people, who have hidden files, hide things from their gurus and are more loyal to their friends who aid them and abet them in their actions. That is the reality, and it results in splits in families, organizations and in society, in turn creating imbalances, strife, confusion, separation, disturbance, anxiety, phobias and distance. Many complain of work pressure, yet this is the actual pressure of life that you must confront. These are the situations of life, and change can only happen if there is a personal desire to improve.

True vision of yoga: integrating head, heart, hands

The vision of Swami Sivananda and of Swami Satyananda is to live yoga in its true spirit and nature. The idea that Swami Sivananda gave on yoga is to cultivate the faculties of head, heart and hands, which combines principles of every aspect of yoga.

There are different needs of the human personality and nature. You cannot cater to the whims of the mind all the time. Just as a wild animal has to be tamed, restrained and brought under control, at some point in life you have to restrain your wild ambitions and aspirations to discover the balance, peace and creativity within. In order to appreciate life you have to construct a qualitative life that connects you with the beauty, the *sundaram*; the good and the bountiful, the *Shivam*; and the eternally existing that does not change, which is the need of each and everyone, the *satyam*. Swami Sivananda saw yoga practices as a means to integrate and awaken the faculties of the head, heart and hands, and as a means to develop a different state of mind, one in which you are connected to the purity of your self and not identified with the distorted visions of life as given by the ego, ambitions and the senses.

20

Ego, desires and senses are the three problem areas of each individual's life; in everybody's life, the senses, the desires and the ego all play a major role. The purpose of sadhana is to harmonize the senses. The purpose of sadhana is to identify the desires and the practicality, reality and actuality of them, and then to use the strength of ego to realize one's Self.

Are you only a desire? You say, 'I am spirit', yet you behave like a desire. There is nothing of spirit in it. There is no logic or understanding; there is only desire. In your life, you live desire, you live the ego and you live the senses. This is how you interact with people, with the environment and with the world, and spirituality is only a concept which you want to learn. Sri Swamiji always said, "Where have you learnt hatred? Where have you learnt jealousy? Where have you learnt aggression? Where have you learnt envy?" They are natural expressions in your life. When you are connected to negativity, then the negative expressions become natural.

You want to learn how to be kind and compassionate, sympathetic and sincere. This has to be a natural expression in life. When you are connected to positivity, the positive actions should become natural, yet it does not happen. Sri Krishna says in the *Bhagavad Gita* that it is easy to have the idea that 'I can be good', however, it is difficult to actually be good. You can believe you are good and hypnotize yourself, thinking, 'I am good, I am good, I am good'. However, what is your bar, what is your parameter, what are your qualifications for being good? Nobody can become good until he or she connects with the positive, creative forces of life.

Swami Sivananda says that just as you make a vegetable tasty, you have to make yoga tasty. You cannot have one kilo of salt in one litre of water, with one kilo of potatoes, one kilo of tomatoes, one kilo of brinjal, one kilo of condiments and expect a nice tasting vegetable. It has to be prepared in ratios: a pinch of salt and a pot of water, a spoonful of masalas and the vegetable. For everything there is a ratio; in yoga too there is a ratio. You cannot practise one hour of asana, one hour of meditation, one hour of yoga nidra and one hour of pranayama.

Yoga must be practised in different ratios, from a pinch to a kilo. If you practise asana for one hour, practise serenity for five minutes every day. If you practise pranayama for twenty minutes, practise satya for ten minutes every day. If you meditate for one hour, bring the peace from your meditation into your active life for at least five minutes every day. A pinch, a few spoonfuls, a litre, a bucketful; the combination has to be appropriate. You will see that in a short time the vegetable becomes enjoyable and tasty. People who come to this stage live yoga naturally all the time, without any effort.

From shore to shore to mushrooming of yoga

During this present age period, Swami Satyananda the crown disciple of Swami Sivananda, received the mandate to teach yoga, to take yoga 'from door to door and shore to shore'. Sri Swamiji did not immediately start his mission like others do. He travelled for nine years to assess the needs of society and to decide on the best way to disseminate the teachings of yoga. He came to the conclusion that yoga should not be taught just as a physical practice, instead as a system to enhance the beauty and the harmony of life. In 1963 he established the Bihar School of Yoga (BSY), and that is when our work started.

Fifty years have passed, and I have had the opportunity to see the first generation of yoga teachers, the second-generation yoga teachers, and to see the mushrooming of yoga teachers. The first generation were people who propagated yoga and conveyed the real knowledge of yoga. The second generation passed on the teachings of their masters and carried the essence forward. Then, when the mushrooming happened, there was a decline in the appreciation of yoga.

Yoga in Europe in the 1960s was leotard yoga: males and females both in leotards, practising dynamic yoga, propagating hatha yoga for trimming the waistline and beautifying the body. The exotic Indian culture had become popular, and all the models of the sixties would wear leotards and 'do yoga', and that is how people were attracted to yoga. Such people were also in Australia in the 1960s, yet there was also an interest in classical yoga there. A strong root of yoga developed in Australia.

Some good teachers and good gurus migrated to the US, the 'land of opportunity', and soon the US became the supermarket of gurus. Even today it is a supermarket of gurus, with many local gurus there. In the 1980s when I was in the US, we were the imported gurus. Now, thousands of local gurus have become overnight prophets with their eyes on profit. This has happened everywhere, and it has brought about a change in how people view yoga.

Yoga research reveals hidden potential

In the 1960s, yoga was seen as a physical culture. In the 1970s, it was seen as a way to overcome stress, anxiety and tension, to focus, to concentrate, and to acquire autonomic control over the body functions. Many sannyasins and yogis were tested to see if they had any type of control over the autonomic body functions. Swami Rama of the Himalaya Institute was tested and he was able to voluntarily stop his heart for a period of eleven minutes, and then again restart it. Swami Nadabrahmananda was able to hold his breath for one hour, which is an impossible feat. I was also tested. By doing a simple meditation I was able to stop my brainwaves. Joe Kamia, leader in alpha research, was my researcher in San Francisco, and he could not believe that somebody could stop their brainwaves. In this way, this second generation of teachers contributed their bit to investigate and demonstrate what is possible and what is not possible.

Swami Niranjanananda
participating in research

In this same period, the USSR and other Communist countries conducted a series of psychic research which was later published in the book, *Psychic Discoveries behind the Iron Curtain*. It was a groundbreaking book, since they were using techniques of yoga, meditation, relaxation and concentration to enhance ESP ability. Research indicated a latent power inherent in every person and in every created form, whether it is a rabbit, a cat, a dog, or a human being. We can communicate telepathically with each other; we can have clairvoyance and clairaudience, and these faculties are awakened by going through the processes of mental training. Sometime later, further research came out of Europe and the US, which presented studies on people who had attempted to awaken their kundalini and chakras and to explore the hidden dimensions.

Rainbow hippies and the craze for self-realization

This was also the period when the drugs like LSD came out; the Woodstock Festival and the hippie movement started. What people do not know is that the inaugurators of the Woodstock Festival in 1968 were two sannyasins: one was Swami Satchidananda of the Integral Yoga Institute in the US, and the other was Swami Satyananda of the Bihar School of Yoga, Munger. Maharishi Mahesh Yogi was the guru of The Beatles at that time, and George Harrison sang the kirtan *Bhajo Radhe Krishna, Gopala Krishna*. This was a period when

Swami Satyananda with Swami Satchidananda, New York, 1968

the spiritual awareness was on the rise, and people wanted to know, 'Is there something different from the material and physical dimension which we are confined in?' There was a lot of interest in meditation, in managing the mind and emotions, and in learning concentration.

Buddhism then came in with meditation, contemplation, compassion and the idea of Buddhahood. Buddhists talk of coming to nirvana, *shoonyata*, nothingness, where the mind stops and there is only stillness. The yogis also say that when the mind stops there is no experience; however, beyond this there is the experience of the higher nature. Beyond the void there is the light, and you have to come to the light. You cannot just stay in limbo, you cannot just stay in a passive state of no activity. There has to be activity by overcoming the lower nature and attaining higher consciousness. That becomes the point of light. When yogis said that there is another stage beyond the void, beyond shoonyata, the interpreters started saying that there is a point of realization where you realize that you are divine. That became the idea of enlightenment and suddenly this idea flashed everywhere: 'You can become self-realized, enlightened'. There was a craze for enlightenment.

Yoga goes viral

After the eighties, when yoga became a more popular household word, two things happened: one, it became the subject of academic research, study and interpretation; and, two, it went viral like a computer virus that goes viral. Suddenly everybody took a week long or month long yogasana teacher training course, read ten asana books and said, "I am a yoga teacher. I will come to your house and teach you yoga." Yoga went viral and this happened everywhere; in the US, in Europe, in South-East Asia, and this trend continues till today.

In this manner people started branding yoga. When yoga became viral, suddenly yoga practices became 'hot yoga', 'cold yoga', 'power yoga'; all different branded yogas came into existence. This is one scenario: yoga went viral. Thousands of people began patenting their own version of yoga, without knowing anything about yoga. Their knowledge has come only from reading twenty asana books, and writing by copying from twenty other books, without any understanding of the yogic systems or personal experience.

Yoga becomes an academic subject

The other aspect is that yoga also became an academic subject studied in universities, and the Bihar School of Yoga was the forerunner of that. Bihar Yoga Bharati (BYB) became the world's first yoga university, officially recognized by the Government of India as a university. We had undergraduate, graduate, and masters courses in yoga philosophy, yoga psychology, applied yogic science, and yoga ecology.

BYB built its own yoga psychology document and its syllabus is now being taught in seven universities in India. Previously the only prevalent psychology was the western approach, which is only a couple of hundred years old from the time of Freud and Jung. What about before them?

Were the earlier human civilizations so idiotic that Freud and Jung had to come forward to show the way? No. There was a previous system of psychology, and it was not a separate subject like it is today; it was an integrated, moral, behavioural, disciplinary subject of the mind. Where there is *sanyam*, you do not need psychological intervention. Where there is no sanyam, you do need psychological intervention. A culture that believes in the principles of sanyam does not need the 'id' of Freud.

BSY and BYB yoga and academic training is also being conducted at Jeju University in Jeju Island, South Korea. Similarly, there is an agreement with a university in Ljubljana, Slovenia, where yoga is being taught in the sports department. The Australian Government has recognized Satyananda Yoga Academy as an RTO, a Registered Training Organization. It is an independent educational organization, which is able to conduct its own programs and syllabuses. Furthermore, yoga has become a subject of study in many colleges and universities. BSY and BYB became the forerunner in the academic field and later many others followed suit.

Shelter for all under the majestic tree of yoga

At present one sees two trends: the viral trend, in which everybody is trying to grab a piece of the yoga pie and gain recognition as a master of yoga; and an academic trend, where research is being done to bring forth the yogic practices for our use today and to understand how to apply them on a day-to-day basis. There are many people in the world who are doing yeoman jobs, commendable jobs, and there are also many people in the world who are riding piggyback on the work being done by others.

Under a tree, a yogi meditates. Under the same tree, a thief comes to divide up the booty. Under the same tree on another side, a tired traveller is fast asleep. The tree is not to be blamed for what happens under its shade. The nature of the tree is to give shade to everybody: a yogi, a crook, a traveller, a child; anybody who needs that shade. It is your intention that uplifts you in wisdom, in action, and in life.

The attempt of yoga is to connect you with that awareness, to identify the real aspiration in your life so that you can attain that fulfilment. If the awareness is there, then yoga is a valuable tool. If the awareness is not there, then it is only a subject of curiosity and you do not change yourself internally, ever. You may cram your intelligence with bookish knowledge, however, that will never convert into experience until and unless you become sincere, serious, and committed, and open your own hidden files.

3

Development of
Satyananda Yoga–Bihar Yoga

Time periods, masters and traditions of yoga

Yoga in the early period was commonly known by the name Pashupata yoga and was divided up into five sub-yogas: mantra yoga, sparsha yoga, bhava yoga, abhava yoga, and maha yoga. Remnants of that lineage are still alive today, and it is known as the Nath tradition of hatha yoga. They are known as kanphata yogis in India, as traditionally they have to pierce their ears. They are the ancient hatha yogis.

Then in the middle period, Pashupata yoga and its aspects were classified. During the middle ages these different yogas were developed by the sages of that age, whose literatures are still available today.

Then the third period, in the present day, the first exposure to yoga came through the British, and the first yogi who exposed yoga to the West was Yogi Rama Charaka. Then, later on came the tradition of kriya yoga, the tradition of Babaji as passed on by Sri Yukteshwar, Lahiri Mahashaya and Paramahamsa Yogananda. The lineage of Krishnamacharya came from Mysore, which was pure, physical hatha yoga. Then came Ramana Maharshi, who brought in jnana yoga. Other people who lived bhakti yoga, like Chaitanya Mahaprabhu, propagated bhakti yoga.

Bhakti yoga actually became a social movement, just like aerobics has now become a social movement. An idea can become a social movement. A practice can become a social

28

movement. Dance and music can become social movements. Anything, according to the time and age, can become a movement if it is accepted by society in large numbers.

There was a period in India when bhakti yoga became a social movement. That was the period of Chaitanya, Kabir, Mirabai and Eknath. From north to south and from east to west, one could see a revival of the bhakti culture, tradition and yoga by these people. How it was interpreted by people was another matter, nonetheless, these bhaktas had attained the highest state. Just as Christ had attained the highest state and yet our interpretation of his teachings do not reflect the accuracy or the intention of his teachings, each one of these saints had also attained a state of realization which they lived, and their thoughts became a social movement.

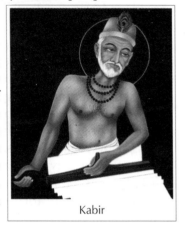

Kabir

Working together in unity for yoga

When Swami Sivananda's tradition came into existence, his disciples took up certain components of yoga, which created a wave. Until the 1940s or 1950s, yoga was seen in a different light from how it is seen today. When I was a child and came to the ashram, people would say, "Why are you practising yoga? It is only for renunciates. It is only for attaining moksha. You have your whole life before you." One was discouraged from adopting yoga, as it was believed to be a discipline for the recluses and renunciates, and not for people of society. If one went out to teach yoga in India, people used to say, "You have come to take us away from our responsibilities," or, "What will yoga do to us except make us more God-oriented?" That is how yoga was seen by society in my youth.

Gradually an interest was generated in society and people got involved. My guru, Swami Satyananda, along with the others like Mr Iyengar, Swami Satchidananda, Swami Vishnudevananda, Swami Venkatesananda, became the first generation of yoga masters whose teachings and traditions of yoga migrated out of India.

In the decades of the seventies, eighties, nineties and two thousand, it was the first and second-generation teachers who spread the word of yoga, thus the authenticity was maintained. People looked at yoga as a way of evolving and progressing in different areas of life, and there was visible social conduct among the teachers as well.

All the first-generation yoga teachers would interact with each other and complement each other with skills and knowledge which the other person did not have. Plans were made together for the coming years of what would be taught by yoga ashrams, yoga centres and teachers. Mr Iyengar, Swami Satyananda, Swami Satchidananda, Swami Vishnudevananda, all interacted. They worked together to create a proper plan for the propagation of yoga that was uniform in all centres and countries.

Research was conducted, teachers were trained, scientific and medical investigations were conducted, specific training programs were formulated, such as stress management for industries and enhancing the learning abilities in children. In the 1980s, when I was in the US, I, along with a Bulgarian scientist, Doctor Lozanov, and Charles Smith from the US, established an organization called SALT: System of Accelerated Learning and Training. We assessed the students and the environment in many schools and colleges to try to improve the method of giving education in classrooms; and it was a success. In this manner, there was a specific and definite plan of progression.

Then the first-generation group retired and passed on the baton to the second generation. Swami Satyananda, my guru, called me back in 1983 and gave me the responsibility of the yoga movement. I followed this mandate for twenty-five years, until 2008. The first-generation disciples of the different traditions became the second-generation yoga propagators. Not teachers; propagators. We were elevated to that post after the retirement of the first generation, while the teaching was taken over by others.

Boom of yoga teachers and yogic studies

The interest spread and everybody wanted to become a yoga teacher. I would always say, "If everyone becomes a teacher, who will be the student?" To maintain the sanctity, plan or project there should be few teachers. You cannot have an Oxford and Harvard in every city and town. It is in one place where the teaching, projects and plans are developed and carried out accordingly by satellite colleges and centres. As it happens, human greed takes over, and the social, economical and financial needs override every other pious intention in life.

In this way, yoga went viral, and at the same time another strong movement emerged: the classical, the academic, the traditional; and it was self-sustaining. In this category, the Government of India recognizes only four yoga centres in India as centres of national importance and national resource. Number one: Sivananda Ashram in the north, in Rishikesh. Number two: Bihar School of Yoga in the east, in Munger. Number three: Vivekananda Kendra in the south, in Bangalore. Number four: Kaivalyadhama in the west, in Lonavla. These are the four organizations – in the north, east, south and west – that the Government of India has officially recognized as centres of yoga in India. These four centres have followed the classical and traditional systems of yoga. Out of these four,

Sivananda Ashram, Rishikesh

Bihar School of Yoga, Munger

Bihar School of Yoga is at the forefront. This is not to advertise the achievements of this institution; it is a fact. The credit for bringing BSY to the top goes to its founder, Swami Satyananda, who brought about a renaissance of yoga in the twentieth century.

Swami Satyananda's contribution to yoga

Sri Swamiji received the instruction from Swami Sivananda to propagate yoga from door to door and shore to shore, and he spent nine years after receiving this mandate working tirelessly to establish the Bihar School of Yoga.

Yoga propagation: During this period of nine years, Sri Swamiji travelled throughout each and every state, town, and village of the Indian subcontinent by foot, on elephantback, camelback, on bullock carts, in boats, in the first cars, the chugging Fords; whatever was available. Sri Swamiji acquainted himself with every area, city, populace and society of India, and realized their requirements and needs. He thought about how yoga could become a tool to manage the human situation. It was from this perspective that he started developing yoga. He furthered the teaching of Swami Sivananda in a synthesized and

Sri Swamiji

integrated manner, which today you recognize as the Bihar Yoga tradition, not system.

Research and classification: Sri Swamiji became the first person to classify yogasanas into forward, backward, inverted, standing and balancing poses. His book, *Asana Pranayama Mudra Bandha (APMB)*, was the first book in the world on yogasanas, pranayamas, mudras and bandhas. In 1968, the first edition of the book was published. If you compare the original edition with the latest edition, you will see that the style of printing, the information, the content, etc. has remained the same and has not changed.

Sri Swamiji did not conduct research into asana; however, he was the first person to research pranayama, pratyahara, dharana and dhyana. Initially everything was clubbed under one name: meditation. Sri Swamiji identified the practices of pratyahara and the other stages of raja yoga. The terms 'pratyahara' and 'dharana' were until recently confined to Patanjali's teachings, without any understanding by the commentators. Commentators, teachers and students would say, "We are practising meditation", a universal, generic term. People did not know what was what. It was Sri Swamiji who wrote the book *Meditations from the Tantras* and first identified the different practices and gave the reasons why they are beneficial and for which mental and emotional conditions. Sri Swamiji identified how the practices could alter each type of mindset, psychology, thought, idea and quality.

Yoga development: Sri Swamiji was the researcher and the developer of yoga nidra, and I was the guinea pig. My education in yoga did not begin with asana and pranayama; it began with yoga nidra, with pratyahara. As I was the guinea pig, all the stages of pratyahara and dharana were tested on me. The book *Yoga Nidra*, mentions how a naughty boy was guided to become a better person.

Sri Swamiji was the first person to define the sequence of stages in antar mouna, ajapa japa, chidakasha dharana, yoga nidra, and the states of pratyahara, dharana and dhyana.

He was the first person to start a postal correspondence course of three years in kriya yoga, in 1973. Never before had the teachings of kriya yoga been written on paper, since it was only an oral tradition between guru and disciple. Today the kriya yoga of Swami Satyananda and the kriya yoga of Paramahamsa Yogananda are the only two kriya yoga systems in the world.

Expressive yoga, connecting the inner and the outer: Sri Swamiji gave a connection to each yoga with life: how it should evolve in life for the betterment and enhancement of human skills, understanding and creativity; he did not limit it to self-realization.

If you think that by coming to the Bihar School of Yoga you can attain moksha, then you have come to the wrong place. Here the philosophy is that you do not run away from life, instead, you run into life with your arms open. That is the training and the teaching. Therefore, if you have come here with the idea of meditation, forget it. There is no meditation here. There is always the emphasis to acquire a better understanding of yourself. At BSY you are made to confront your inner enemies: hatred, jealousy, anger, frustration, ego, passion, desire and greed. At the same time you are also given the opportunity to express the qualitative you. How much you do is up to you, however, that opportunity is always given in equal measure.

There is a story of two dogs; one is black and the other is white. They are your dogs. The black dog is the baddie: tamasic, negative, bad, dominant, all the best of the negative is in the black dog. The white dog is the goody and all the best of the positive is in the white dog. These two dogs fight with each other. Which dog will win? The dog that you feed more will win, and that is the reality in life too.

You live with these two dogs and the dog that you feed more wins the fight. The choice of which dog to feed is yours, however, they are both with you. They are both within your body, mind and heart. Which dog you feed is your choice in life, whether spiritual life or social life. Those who feed the positive, the white one, and make it stronger are in a better position to reach the pinnacle of life and understand what the whole game is about. Those who feed the negative, the black dog, live their life in frustration, anxiety, nervous tension, fear and insecurity. Thus, the purpose of Sri Swamiji's yoga became a way to explore the inherent human potential.

Progressive sequence through sadhana: In Sri Swamiji's system of yoga he has combined the principles and attitudes of tantra and Vedanta as well. In the sequence of progression in sadhana, he identified hatha yoga as asana, pranayama, mudra, bandha and shatkarmas. He was the first person to write on *bandhas*, the psychic locks. He was the first person to explain the *mudras*, psychic gestures. In raja yoga, Sri Swamiji defined and explained pranayama, pratyahara, dharana and dhyana.

He developed kriya yoga as the third movement. First, there was hatha yoga for body and prana: annamaya kosha and pranamaya kosha. Next, raja yoga for mind and consciousness: manomaya kosha and vijnanamaya kosha. Third, kriya yoga for exploring the inner potential, the inner psychic awakening, leading to the experience of anandamaya kosha as the completeness, the fullness, the total.

These three were complemented with the inclusion of the other yogas such as mantra yoga, nada yoga, swara yoga, kundalini yoga, etc. He also defined bhakti yoga, jnana yoga and karma yoga as the expressive yoga. In that, he gave a message: that the purpose of yoga is to move from self-oriented absorption in oneself to selfless, expanded awareness of everyone. This became his teaching and thus the teaching of Bihar Yoga.

Teachings for an awakened, creative nature: In this age, it is Swami Satyananda who has done hard work to make yoga accessible to everyone in a systematic and scientific manner. For this, he has a position higher than Patanjali, Gheranda or anybody else, since he has looked at every aspect and angle of yoga. That is what you receive today, and you will continue to receive in the future as well. Other propagators have only given us one teaching, whereas Sri Swamiji has given teachings on all the yogas, in addition to incorporating the attitudes of Vedanta and tantra into the practical application of yoga in life.

The teachings of Swami Sivananda's 18 ITIES in the form of serenity, regularity, absence of vanity, and so on; the SWAN theory: strengths, weaknesses, ambitions and needs – are all yogic practices to develop, harmonize and regulate self-expression. Once that self-expression is correct, then you are free, creative and content. It is correct self-expression, right expression at all levels that indicates the awakened, creative nature.

4

Hallmarks of
Satyananda Yoga–Bihar Yoga

There are different identifying marks of the Satyananda Yoga–Bihar Yoga tradition, and to know these you must understand how Swami Sivananda taught yoga to Swami Satyananda.

The pinnacle: kriya yoga

Not everybody in Swami Sivananda's ashram learnt yoga. Some were teachers, some were administrators, some were workers in the different departments and areas, so there was no formal learning time. The same is applicable in Munger. Not everyone here is a yogi or yoga teacher. Some are workers, some are administrators, and some are teachers. Therefore, do not think that every geru-wearer is a master, or teacher of yoga just because they live here.

Sri Swamiji practising kriya yoga

When Swami Sivananda gave the mandate to Swami Satyananda to spread yoga from door to door and shore to shore, Sri Swamiji said, "You have given me this instruction, but I do not know any yoga. I have been busy in the kitchen,

37

in publications, in administration, as a secretary, as a well-digger. I have done everything except yoga, and now you have given me this order." Swami Sivananda said, "Come with me." He took him to his room, and in fifteen minutes initiated Sri Swamiji in kriya yoga through shaktipat. *Shaktipat* is transmission.

Kriya yoga was the yoga that Sri Swamiji learnt from Swami Sivananda; and Swami Sivananda told him that the finality of all yoga is kriya yoga. Kriya yoga became the focus of the Satyananda Yoga–Bihar Yoga tradition. No matter what you do, whether you start with hatha yoga, raja yoga, jnana yoga, bhakti yoga, kundalini yoga or mantra yoga, you have to eventually come to kriya yoga in order to become stable in your life and in your spiritual experience. Kriya yoga has become the goal of the Satyananda Yoga–Bihar Yoga tradition. That is point one.

Transmission yoga

The second point, which I have noticed and many of you have also noticed in your own life, is the role of transmission. People hear of shaktipat, the transmission that takes place between guru and disciple. What is this shaktipat? It is generally said to be the transference of spiritual power from one person to another. How can it be understood in a language? The language to understand this process is that of computers.

You have a hard drive full of information. You get another hard drive and you download the information on the first hard drive on to this second hard drive. That downloading is known as 'transmission'. When the new, second disk receives the information, it becomes a replica of the first, original disk. The new disk has the same information. In one instant the whole of the information contained on the original disk, which took years to collect, is transferred. The new disk contains the exact replica of the content from the other disk. It is not a copy; it is a replica. This illustrates shaktipat.

A capable guru can transmit *jnana*, knowledge, to a capable disciple; not to every disciple, only to the capable disciple. Once the capable disciple receives the transmission, that disciple becomes the replica of the guru. The same information contained in the guru's mind is transmitted to the disciple's mind. This transmission has also become a hallmark of the Satyananda Yoga tradition, inexplicable as it is.

Sri Swamiji transmitting the shakti

When the disciples of BSY go to teach and allow that guru inspiration to come through, they become the best teachers. How this happens cannot be explained; nevertheless, it is an experience of many teachers in this tradition. Many new people who went on yoga yatras in 2013 reported that experience on their return. When they teach and follow their inner instinct, at that time they become the conduit for the teaching that is inherent, contained within, and it flows through. In the normal state they are not able to answer the most simple, basic question, but in that state of transmission they can answer all enquiries. In that state the information simply flows, and this has also become a hallmark of the Satyananda Yoga tradition.

I also experience it from time to time: the downloading of information, the flow of understanding received from the masters. I am not using the word 'knowledge' since anybody can repeat knowledge. I am using the word 'understanding'. Something that emerges from understanding is unique and special. This is shaktipat; this is the transmission that is inherent in this tradition.

Understanding the mental dimension

Another salient point of this tradition is the focus on the mental aspect of yoga. The mind is something that people

39

generally do not understand or even realize they have. Whenever you have any mental problems or conflicts, you instantly seek a distraction outside and you never face your own problems and difficulties. Whenever there is any type of problem in the mind, whether it is anxiety, frustration, nervousness, depression, aggression, jealousy, love, compassion or sympathy, whatever state, you do not acknowledge it within yourself; you look for a reference point outside. Whenever there is any problem you avoid that problem by looking in some other direction. The mind has become the subject for psychiatrists and psychologists to deal with and treat as you think, 'When there is a crisis I will go to them. Until then, I will not worry about it.'

Nobody worries about their body until they are sick, and nobody realizes they have a mind until they reach a mental crisis. Due to this situation, especially in the West, people find different practices of pratyahara, relaxation or yoga nidra quite confronting and challenging, since they are never aware of themselves. Many times people become aware of their heart palpitation in yoga nidra and get frightened. They realize for the first time in their life that something is beating inside their ribcage. This frightens them and they say, "My heart is beating very hard and fast!" For the first time in their life they have observed their heartbeat and then conclude that it is beating hard and fast, though it is simply that they did not have any awareness of it prior to that moment. In the state of relaxation or concentration, any event that is in the mind or in the memory is suddenly released, it flashes before one's awareness and triggers off certain emotions or responses caused by that event. Many people do not like it and say it is challenging and confronting.

In the West and now also in the East, people are reaching a point where they are actually disconnecting from their own mental and emotional expressions and experiences. They try to avoid these mental and emotional feelings contained within themselves and do not acknowledge them. When it comes to yoga, you are meditating and suddenly you feel disturbed, as something is coming out. Your rational mind says, 'Suppress it! It'll bring you pain', however, your practice is clearing it. You say, "Oh, it is too confronting. Too challenging; not for me." It even happens in pranayama. When people become aware of their breath they start to suffocate. Suddenly they realize that they are breathing and it brings in fear. Whenever they become aware of the breath they start suffocating and feel that they are not breathing enough. This is an imaginative state of the mind that manifests when you suddenly realize you are something more than what you had perceived until now.

There are other types of people who do not go through this kind of mental crisis and who are happy and free. Even these carefree people suffer as they see other people expressing pain and anxiety, and wonder, "Why am I happy? Something must be wrong with me! Maybe it is not being released from within. Maybe I'm not getting free; I'm holding on too tightly to my blocks." Then they go into a different type of crisis.

This is another reason why people identify more with yogasanas and less with meditation. Meditation has become a tool to distract the mind from problems, and not to confront the mind. Meditating to clear one's stress is only a superficial approach. People also use meditation to go on an imaginative journey, seeing angels and lights and all the fantasies that they can conjure up. Who uses meditation to enhance the ability of their mind? Few people make the effort to discover their own mind. In society today, people have not experienced or realized their mind.

Discovering the mind

The focus of Bihar Yoga is not only on asana in hatha yoga; it is on all aspects of hatha yoga. The emphasis is not the physical aspects only; there is more emphasis on the pranic, since the physical is a representation of the pranic condition. If you are sick physically, the pranas are depleted. In hatha yoga, the Satyananda Yoga tradition looks to balancing, awakening and activating prana with the use of yogasanas. Similarly, in raja yoga this tradition looks at the components of yama and niyama, along with pratyahara, dharana and dhyana; and the asana and pranayama are used as tools to internalize. There is a definite effort to discover one's mind, and that is where people find the biggest challenge, whether they be the modern sannyasins or yoga practitioners.

Swami Sivananda, Swami Satyananda and Bihar Yoga are clear that if you want happiness, completeness and wholeness in life, this mind has to be managed properly. Sri Swamiji says, "If you have a fight with your wife or children in your home, you can sleep in separate rooms and have a good night's sleep. However, if you fight with your mind, where will you put your mind? You can't put your mind in a separate room; it will sleep with you! It will wake with you! It will talk to you. It will create problems for you. It will keep you awake the whole night. So it is better to keep this mind happy. If this mind is happy, you can live your life in a happy manner."

In all the teachings of Sri Swamiji, he has placed emphasis on the mind. In all the teachings of Swami Sivananda, he has placed emphasis on developing the positive qualities of the mind and eradicating the negative and restrictive qualities of the mind. That has been the teaching, for through the mind you can experience your awakened nature.

Understanding the real and the unreal

Many exponents of yoga say the experiences of the mind are unreal, whereas many exponents of yoga say the experiences of the mind are real. Who to believe? If the experiences of the mind are unreal, then even the idea of *shanti*, peace, that you experience in your mind is unreal. The happiness that you experience in your mind is unreal.

If all the experiences of the mind are real, then there is no negation of anything and there cannot be any change, as it is the same pattern of suffering, happiness, struggle, behaviour, expectation and desire. The patterns of behaviour, expectation, needs and desires do not change. In childhood you play with little toy cars. When you get some money you play with real cars and get a new car every six months or every year. When you are young you play with little dolls, little he-dolls and she-dolls, and when you grow up you play with bigger he-dolls and she-dolls. You also change them many times according to your likes, fights and choices. Maybe you have lived a life like this, too.

One student from India went to the US. In a group interview, they were discussing the family. These people were asked to make a map of their family: mother, father, brother, sister, and so on. The Indian student got up and drew father, mother, son and daughter, and that was the family that she came from. Everybody in the class observed her and commented, "You have only a single pair of parents? Really?" When they were doing their exercise, another girl put up the image of her first mother, then her stepmother, then the second stepmother; then the father, then stepfather, and another stepfather. Then all the cousins and everybody that came under them, and brothers and sisters. That was their idea of family. The person from India was the only one who had the minimum square: mother, father, brother, sister; finished. The other images showed two mothers, two fathers, or even more.

In relation to the mind, what is reality and what is illusion? When you begin to think of yourself as a reality or illusion you miss the point. Swami Sivananda says: "Improve your present by learning from the past, and develop strength and hope for the future." You live in the present; your body, brain and mind are in the present. Yet your mind is always lost in the past, and your fears and insecurities are always about the future. You never enjoy the present, as you live in your memories of the past, are fearful of your future and ignore your present. In this situation any experience of the mind is false; it is unreal, as it does not ground you in the present condition and present reality. When you use the learning from the past to improve and excel in the present, and to be optimistic for the future, then that experience of the mind becomes real. This is how the tantras and the Upanishads describe the experience of the real and the unreal in life.

It is not a question of intellectual, philosophical analysis or understanding. It is simply a realization that when you use the learning from the past to excel in the present then that expression, that life, that state of being is the real you. Whatever you experience at that moment is real. If, though, you are ignoring your present by living in your past memories, and you are apprehensive, fearful, insecure or uncertain about your future, then any type of experience that you have will not be the present, correct one. According to tantra, getting lost in either the past or the future is unreal, while focusing on the present is real.

This is also the progression in the mental awareness of yoga: pratyahara, dharana and dhyana. As previously mentioned, three yogas are considered important: hatha yoga for annamaya and pranamaya kosha, raja yoga for manomaya and vijnanamaya kosha, and kriya yoga for anandamaya kosha. Yoga in this

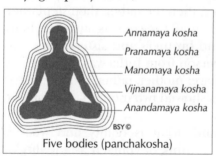

Annamaya kosha
Pranamaya kosha
Manomaya kosha
Vijnanamaya kosha
Anandamaya kosha

BSY©

Five bodies (panchakosha)

44

context is a journey and exploration of the five sheaths, the five bodies, the five expressions of life, and enhancement of one's ability.

Children and yoga

The benefits of yoga are more visible in children than in adults. When children adopt yoga they do it in a natural and spontaneous manner, while adults come to yoga with certain expectations and needs. Once the expectations and needs are fulfilled, their association with yoga ends. Yoga does not

BYMM children teaching yoga

become a part of their culture in life, whereas in a child's life whatever they learn becomes a part of their future expression later on in life. It happens in a natural and spontaneous manner. As a yoga teacher, one should focus on bringing this yogic understanding to the little ones and not wait until they reach a point of crisis in their life. That has been our experience.

When we bring yoga to children and see them grow up and join different professional areas and take on different responsibilities, there is a marked difference between them and other children who have not had the yogic exposure. A definite, clear difference can be seen between the two groups of people: the yoga group and the non-yoga group. Therefore, in Bihar Yoga there is strong emphasis on teaching yoga to children in India and elsewhere.

Yoga around the globe

In Europe we have an organization called RYE, located in Paris. The RYE movement has existed since 1976, and its job is to teach yoga in schools and colleges. In October last year, the Department of Education, Government of France, gave a statement that the Bihar Yoga system will be taught in all the educational institutions of the country. Now the Satyananda Yoga–Bihar Yoga system is official in the schools and colleges of France.

Similarly in other countries, yoga is being taught to improve the ability of students to deal with the pressures of education and society, and to find a direction in their life. In 2000, the Bihar Yoga system was introduced by UNESCO in seventeen European countries.

Yoga has come into many other countries. On the American continent there is a society known as Yoga Education Society (YES), whose head office is based in Canada. They publish books for children and distribute the books throughout the US and Canada. You will find *Yoga Education for Children*, Volumes 1 and 2, in schools in North America.

For all of the work done in yoga, the focus and emphasis is on educating the young generation in the disciplines of yoga. If they can imbibe the culture, the discipline, the balance and the harmony that yoga aims to provide, our future will certainly be bright; better than what it is today.

Reaching out to the whole community

In this manner, yoga has reached out from the ashram to many areas. Even in the army, soldiers are given yoga to enhance their creative ability. They are not fighting all the time, they only serve in the army. Yoga is not being taught in the army to make them into a better fighting force, but to increase and enhance their creative human ability. After all, they are the young generation of the nation. They need the direction, help, support and care that any other person in society needs.

In the state of Bihar, we have been teaching the principles of yoga therapy in six medical colleges, to the MBBS students and professors. In response to a request by the Health Department, the Yoga Publications Trust also published a book, *Yogic Management of Common Diseases*, to aid the medical fraternity to use yoga. Once upon a time in Australia in 1976,

1977, 1978, doctors would prescribe medication, and in the same prescription write the relevant yoga practices for you to do. You had a choice to take medicine or yoga. Of course, when yoga went viral, all these things stopped, as the results were not good. Many of the activities that happened in the early seventies and eighties are not happening now due to yoga going viral and people losing touch with the tradition and only identifying yoga as a physical practice. However, if yoga is practised in a systematic manner, a positive change in life and in society is possible.

A classical and traditional system

The Bihar Yoga tradition developed over a period of time with the understanding that human nature has to be cultivated homogeneously. With that awareness in mind, it is one of the most classical and traditional systems of yoga at present in the world. Learning and mastering are different: learning does not take time; mastering takes time. You also have to experience the benefit that yoga can give so you can be convinced yourself. If you yourself are convinced you will be benefited, whether it be spiritual benefit or commercial benefit. If you are convinced you will also gain commercially, as you will put your heart and soul into it and you will become a good yoga teacher. Both ways are good.

5

Living Yoga at the Gurukul

Another aspect of the Bihar Yoga tradition is ashram life, which is an important facet for those who want to explore yoga in a different environment. All the courses at the Bihar School of Yoga are residential; there are no day courses.

My guru, Swami Satyananda, once said to me, "It does not do justice to yoga when people come to study yoga for one hour and then go back to their homes and live an undisciplined life. Yoga education cannot be imparted in that manner. Therefore at BSY there should only be residential courses." This was his guideline right from the beginning.

Following this mandate and the system of the residential ashram structure that Sri Swamiji developed, gurukul living became an important aspect of learning yoga. You may have also seen for yourself that when you first came to Ganga Darshan, you did not find yourself in a yoga centre; you came to a place where three different traditions merge together.

Confluence of three traditions

Ganga Darshan is a confluence where the three traditions – yoga, the gurukul lifestyle and sannyasa – merge together.

Yoga: One teaching is that of yoga; people come here for yoga training, they stay for the duration of the course and then they go back. Their association and main concern is yoga. That is one aspect of this place.

Gurukul lifestyle: The second aspect is gurukul living; ashram living, communal living. What is the foundation of this lifestyle? Togetherness is the foundation of ashram living. It is not individual growth but communal growth that is encouraged in the ashram. My wish is that everybody respect,

Yogic Studies

honour and cooperate with each other. These are the components of the gurukul tradition, where one learns accountability and understanding in real life. In the gurukul, one lives the yamas and the niyamas, and makes the effort to transcend and overcome the limitations that hold one back. That aspect is known as ashram living or the gurukul tradition.

In the past, in the times of Rama and Krishna, they lived in the gurukul like normal people, forgetting their status and position, and lived with one *bhava*, with one attitude: 'We are working together to further the mission of the tradition and guru. We are not working to enhance our own prestige and position.' With this idea even Rama, Krishna and the children of emperors lived with the children of poor people and developed understanding, awareness, sympathy, affection, and a sense of help and cooperation. This is gurukul life in the ashram, where a personal discipline is imbibed to connect with wisdom, not with the ego and the detrimental mental qualities. That is the purpose of ashram living, which is the second tradition.

Sannyasa: The third tradition is sannyasa. Sannyasa is a life dedicated to discovering the beauty and the wisdom within oneself. Sannyasa is self-effort.

49

There is the story of a man who bought a deserted, barren piece of land. Nothing grew on that land, except for weeds and rocks that had made it their home. Not a single blade of grass was a tenant there. After purchasing the piece of land this man worked hard, day and night, to clear, prepare, till and plant flowers, fruit and trees on the land. In the course of time he made that barren, rocky piece of land into a beautiful garden, which became famous. The fame of this garden's beauty invited people from all over the land to admire it, just as people go to Disneyland and Disneyworld.

One day a priest came and was wonderstruck by the beauty of the garden. While he was walking around, he exclaimed, "What a wonderful creation of God this is! Such beauty! Such peace! Such tranquillity! Such attraction! It's so colourful!" The gardener, who was walking with the priest and showing him the garden, said, "Sorry, I disagree with you. This is my hard work. You should have seen this piece of land when God was its owner! Nothing used to grow here except rocks and weeds. It was my effort and hard work that made this land into a beautiful garden." That is sannyasa.

Think about how much rubbish you have cleared out from within yourself, and you will realize where you are in sannyasa. The ability to remove the weeds and the rocks, and to convert the barren piece of land into a beautiful garden is the sannyasa tradition. These three traditions of yoga, ashram life and sannyasa merge at Ganga Darshan.

Ashram life: bringing alive the disciplines of yoga

Common to both the yoga people and the sannyasa people is ashram life, since ashram life is based on disciplines that are referred to in ayurveda, in the Upanishads, in the Vedas and in the tantras. The disciplines here are not self-created. If you have the eyes to see and the wisdom to understand, you will discover that each system placed here, and which has been in place since a long time, represents an aspect of ashram living as enunciated in the tradition.

A recent example: from Guru Poornima to August, for one month breakfast is stopped in the ashram. Many people cannot tolerate it. They think, 'Swamiji has stopped our breakfast.' Some people even ask: 'Why am I being denied my morning breakfast?' They do not recall that we do that every year, since, according to the rules of ayurveda, a one-month period during the monsoon season should be without breakfast for health purposes. Episodes like this, which people believe to be odd decisions of the guru, the management or the administration, are based on principles of ayurveda, disciplines of the Upanishads, the Vedas and the tantras. They are not my whims, neither the whims of my guru nor the whims of Swami Sivananda.

Overcoming the attachment to daily comforts

Today you are accustomed to comforts and you face difficulty when you live in an environment where you have to be responsible for your own things, clean your room and live with strangers; things which you have not done before, yet you have to do at the ashram. The emphasis on cleanliness and order is not an ashram discipline only; it is *shaucha*, the first niyama of Patanjali's *Yoga Sutras*. It is easy to talk about shaucha as a philosophy and not live it in real life. If you keep unwashed glasses in your room and speak of shaucha, it is hypocrisy. At home you can throw your things here, there and everywhere. If you come to the ashram for even fifteen days your roommate is somebody from another part of the world who is a total stranger, and you have to share the room. Therefore, you must keep your room properly and learn the discipline of maintaining yourself.

Why is it difficult to keep clothes properly and fold them neatly? Does it take hours to do that? It takes seconds. You cannot invest even seconds to do something proper and make your bed. How much time does it take to straighten out bedsheets? It doesn't take an hour. When you don't make your bed you excuse yourself and say, "I did not have the time." You don't have thirty seconds to make your bed? Instead, you are

51

willing to accept your laziness and justify your weakness by giving the excuse that you did not have the time. That is not adherence to shaucha; it is an excuse to avoid following the mandate of shaucha. If you do not keep your things neatly in the closet or in other places, how can you consider yourself to be a teacher of shaucha? You have no right to speak on yoga. If you cannot live yoga, you have no right to speak on yoga.

These rules and guidelines are all part of ashram living. Instead of appreciating and trying to understand that, in your search for comfort you try to modify that discipline and system. An example: *mouna*, silence. It is a tradition, yet who follows it? People in geru? Students? Guests? Does anybody truthfully follow it? Although it has been in place for years, it is seen as a restriction, not as a yogic teaching. These are the challenges of ashram life. Non-adherence to the ashram culture represents a disturbed, distracted and dissipated mind; an immature and lethargic mind.

Fusion of action and intention

Why is it difficult for you to feel a sense of belonging and a sense of duty and responsibility? These are in place for your own betterment. In theory everything sounds good to you, however, in practice there is resistance. Sri Swamiji says, "There is always a split between what people think and what they do." This is the cause of conflict, frustration, tension and anxiety. There is a difference between what you think, what you believe and how you perform and act; they are never compatible. When idea and action get fused in the life of an individual, that person becomes a model from whom others take inspiration.

Therefore the learning in ashram life is the union or coming together of intention and action. If the intention is cooperation then action has to be cooperative and should not be guided by your mind, ego, ambition, negativity or positivity. Just as an arrow flies true to its mark without deviation, without turning left or right, human intention and action should have a clear focus when performed. Action has to be like an arrow, based on wisdom and understanding; not on ambition or on petty thinking. Thinking in life should be: 'God, help me to maintain my true direction in life. Let me begin my day like a new day that I've never lived before, and not carry the memories of the past, which restrict my happiness and joy today.' That is my prayer.

If you observe yourself objectively and cultivate humility and understanding, then you can consider that the purpose of ashram life is attainable; just simple understanding, simple cooperation and a simple smile. Swami Sivananda says, "Eat a little, drink a little, smile a little, frown a little, laugh a little, dance a little, sleep a little, meditate a little, do asana a little." For him everything was in little doses. In your case you take a big dose all the time. When you are happy you want to collect all the happiness; when you are angry you want to collect all the aggression, not just a little bit. By cultivating little things, little by little you become big. After all, the ocean is made up of little drops of water.

Discovering the real self by clearing the rubbish

Sannyasa is the cultivation of the garden; ashram life is imbibing the yamas and the niyamas and a positive culture. Naturally when you are cleaning a drain, the rubbish comes out; that does not mean that you are the rubbish. The rubbish that accumulates in the drain is only there for the reason that you have never cleaned it. If it is kept clean, there will not be any accumulation of rubbish. You have to learn how to clean your mind just as your body follows a natural course of correction; you eat and you expel. In the same manner, the mind should also absorb and release. If it

Karma yoga

releases, then moments later you are a normal, happy person. If it does not release, then you can be struggling for years with the stress and anxiety of something that happened years ago.

The yamas and niyamas, and the guidelines that Swami Sivananda has given that you sing, "Serenity, regularity, absence of vanity . . .", the 18 ITIES, are what? Are they only the ramblings of a God-intoxicated saint or do they have some relevance in your life? They form a part of ashram living. The yamas, the niyamas, the vedantic and yogic principles underlie ashram living. You have to constantly and continuously remember this.

Swami Sivananda says, and Sri Krishna in the *Bhagavad Gita* says, it is difficult to do the right thing and easy to do the wrong thing. To do the right thing there has to be proper understanding, analysis and awareness in which the negative never becomes perceived as a mountain; it only becomes a speck of dust. People see the negative as a mountain; however, it is only a speck of dust. What is the cause when a simple problem that should be like a speck of dust is perceived as a mountain? Ego, and your reaction to it. If there is no ego and no reaction, that problem will not even exist.

What is the role of a hospital? You go to hospital to get healthy. However, at hospital you do not see health anywhere. You only encounter disease, viruses, bacteria, big injections and big machines; nothing indicates any symptom of health there. In the doctor's clinic you will not see health anywhere, although people go to the doctor to get healthy. You will only see disease. Health is the outcome of managing the diseased condition. In the same manner, wisdom, understanding and peace are the outcomes of managing the conditions of the mind and ego.

Tools of yama and niyama
In this life that you are born with, you have been given the necessary tools, yet you have never utilized them to discover

your real self. So much time has passed that you have even forgotten how to use those tools, and have instead identified with your ego. The ego does not allow you to use the tools, since it is a virus itself. The ego is not a doctor; it is a virus. The doctor is your intention and your action coming together. When you find this doctor then healing can begin. In order to bring intention and action together, the yamas and niyamas are used. Patanjali has described only five for his purpose; however, yamas and niyamas are contained in every yoga, not just the raja yoga system. Hatha yoga, bhakti yoga, and other yogas have identified different yamas and niyamas according to their purposes. In the yogic literature there are many other yamas and niyamas.

Each yama and niyama relates to the development of one aspect of your nature, cultivating one flower in your mind. In ashram life it is the identification with this that is important. All the other stuff that keeps happening due to the perspective and the identification with your own ego is irrelevant. The problem will not even exist if there is no ego and no reaction. In the same manner, how you react in your mind is your nature, yet it is not the nature of ashram life. The nature of ashram life is to make you aware of different seeds that you can plant in your mind in the form of the yamas and niyamas of yoga, the Vedas and tantra.

In this process of clearing the land, be ready to remove the rocks. Hold them in your hand and look at them objectively and then throw them away. Be ready to pull the weeds, which have large roots reaching into the ground. Although they look small on the top, weeds have huge roots. You have to pull them out. There is no need to fear this; you are recognizing the limiting, restricting and containing quality in yourself. Why be afraid, fearful or insecure about that? Rather, you should be happy that, 'Today I was able to eradicate my jealousy, and now I can cultivate the seed of love.' To be fearful about feeling jealous and going into panic about it is a useless behaviour of the mind.

Instead of identifying with the negative, be happy that now you have the opportunity to do something better and more positive. This is the purpose of ashram life. How you face your negativity is your head-trip, as that is your response to a yama or a niyama, such as shaucha. How you maintain your closet and room is your response to the idea of shaucha. If I go walking around the ashram and say, "It is dirty here. Please clear it up", it is not that I am trying to force something on you; it is making you aware that you are living in an incorrect manner in a place where you have the opportunity to learn to live correctly.

Let Thy will be done

The state of realization is when an idea becomes a sadhana, and does not remain mere intellectual concept, guiding the actions and the behaviours of life. Learn simply how to look, how to hear, how to use the hands, how to use the heart, and what the purpose is in using all the sense faculties. After all, the senses are the form of tejas.

Tejas means fire, luminosity, warmth. Senses without tejas are ineffective; and senses with tejas become the active principle. Tejas is material and transcendental both. When you offer tejas and the sensory connection to the world, they feed ego, hatred, jealousy, aspirations, needs, connections and relationships based on mundane, physical and sensorial ideas and identities. When tejas, awareness and the focus of the senses are given a goal to associate with, and the senses begin to identify with that higher goal and higher nature, that is the real conversion of an idea into an action. When you are looking for beauty, peace, harmony, cooperation and generating sync in unity, then ego, hatred, mind, jealousies, greed, everything has to be left behind, and you have to connect with the spirit of the divine.

You have to become humble. You have to become free from your own obsessions. This humility eventually manifests the awareness of the higher reality, that 'I am only an instrument in the hands of the higher power'. Humility brings forth the realization, 'Let Thy will be done'. Humility brings the understanding that we move together, many people as one, and not create a division between two. When your senses begin to function in that manner, this is the state of Ishwara pranidhana. It is Ishwara pranidhana when the eyes look at the beauty, when the ears listen to the harmony, when the hands reach out to help and not to grab, when the feet do not falter and instead walk towards excellence and perfection, and when the heart is open to love.

This awareness has to be cultivated by following the yamas and niyamas. It is not a challenge to confront one's mind. It is challenging to connect with positivity and that is the purpose of ashram life: to identify what is positive and to connect with that.

6

Three Stages of Practising Yoga

I see the practice of yoga and what it does to the practitioner in three stages. First it is a physical practice, second it is self-discovery, and third it is awakening your creative potential by the energy of grace.

Three progressive stages of yoga
At the first level, as a physical practice, many people do yoga like aerobics, many people do it dynamically, many people do it gently, many people do it consciously and slowly. This is the learning and practice that you do in a studio, in a jungle, in a forest, at home, in the ashram. You experience the body, the pose, the inside of the body, the breathing, the awareness of body. Whatever the manner you practise, the yoga practices influence the body, free up the stiffness and tensions of the body and make you feel more energetic, relaxed, free and light. That is the first level of yoga experience.

The second level of yoga experience involves connecting with yourself. In this stage, you combine different practices and systems to create the right, tasty vegetable. You know the example of cooking tasty vegetables: so much quantity of water, of salt, of condiments and of vegetables, all in proper proportion to each other. When you do yoga in this manner you get in touch with yourself: with your nature, with your personality, and with your body-mind unit together as a whole. What you have been learning here at the Bihar School of Yoga is an indication for the second stage, in order to begin your journey to connect with and realize yourself.

If you recall the things that you have done in the classes taught here: breathing has been combined with posture; mantra has been combined with posture; movement has been combined with posture. When yoga is practised in this manner, any experience taking place in your body is not alien to you; rather, you are able to identify what is happening within yourself. There is a deeper awareness of what your physical body is capable of; of how you can de-stress the mind; of how you can relax; of how you can breathe better; of how you can focus and concentrate better. This awareness makes you aware of your own expressions, and how to modify and rectify them. This is the beginning.

Then there is the third stage of yoga, which is spiritual. The conductors of human creativity awaken and the channels of human receptivity open completely. The dormant faculties awaken. Your creativity develops and you become a channel for the guru's energy or for God's energy in whatever way you express it or feel it.

I will focus on the second aspect, as most are familiar with the first aspect of yoga. The second definition of yoga is also associated with the third stage of yoga.

Second stage of yoga practice: realizing your nature

In the second stage of yoga practice, a deepening of awareness takes you through to the realization of your nature. At present your nature is conditioned, formed and preset, with little scope to change or improve until you really want to. You have to ask yourself, "Do I really want to change?" Most people do not want to change, although they like hearing about it. They like it as a lofty ideal, yet when it comes to their own life they are unable to change it. Why? Human conditioning is like a habit. How do you spell 'habit'? H-A-B-I-T. If you want to remove a habit, what do you do? You remove the H first, then 'a bit' remains. Then you remove A, and 'bit' remains. Then you remove B, and 'it' remains.

This is a vicious circle in life. When you reach the last point you discover that a habit still continues to exist; the conditioning, the form, the shape, the understanding, the container that you live in is still there. The outer garb remains, although inside it is hollow. The formed, determined, preset conditioning is what you are in your mentality, character, knowledge, expression, skill and understanding. These are different in each individual and you do not think in a similar manner.

How can experience take place in yoga when positive ideas are held only as lofty ideals? For example, if I say that anger is bad and it is like a deep well in which you fall and cannot come out again, you will nod your head and say, "Yes, correct, it is really like a deep hole. Oh yes, if I get angry then it is very difficult for me to extract myself from that depth. Swamiji is right." However, you have not realized that anger is a deep hole and you should not fall into it; you have only heard it. If you had realized it, you would make the effort to ensure not to fall in the pit again. That realization is absent. The same thing happens with envy, jealousy, hatred; and same with love, compassion and sympathy.

Whatever you identify with in your life is your clinging post and you do not realize that it is a pit. You go to that pit every day until the realization dawns, "Yes, for the last twenty years I did not realize it was wrong, for I never identified it. It was only a lofty ideal. For twenty years I've been hearing that this is wrong, and today I am realizing that it is wrong." When you get a slap in the face, and you feel the agony and the pain, then you realize that it was not a lofty ideal. It was a pit in which you took shelter every day of your life that

60

you had to avoid, yet you did not. This happens in virtually everyone's life.

Overcoming pitfalls

I have seen people who have succeeded when they have identified these pits and avoided them. When your awareness deepens, you become aware of your conditioning, habits, nature, traits, behaviour, skills, abilities and needs; everything. That is how you connect with the body, with the mind and with life. In this context, yoga practice is not only aerobic exercise; it becomes a tool to connect with the body-mind unit and with life. That is the second stage. The effort of the second stage is not physical; it is not hatha yoga. On the contrary, the effort of the second stage is raja yoga: to connect with the body-mind unit.

The first aspect, the deepening physical awareness, learning and practice that you do as physical exercise, can be related to hatha yoga. The second aspect of yoga experience is the deepening awareness, which can be associated with raja yoga, as it deals with the inner personality, the inner nature. You realize your conditioning, and developing a new set of positive traits, habits and conditioning, you alter the old, detrimental and restrictive into strength and something qualitatively better. Patanjali was clear in his exposition that raja yoga must begin from the basics; not from Ishwara pranidhana, but from shaucha. Ishwara pranidhana is the fifth niyama. You have not started with the first. Ahimsa, satya, asteya, aparigraha and brahmacharya are the five yamas. Shaucha, santosha, tapas, swadhyaya and Ishwara pranidhana are the five niyamas. Until and unless you pass the first class, the second class and so on, you cannot achieve the fifth class. Therefore, in the *Yoga Sutras*, Patanjali has been clear about the steps to a gradual discovery of yourself.

Building a foundation by perfecting the basics

At the second stage of yoga practice is the fine-tuning of your external mental behaviour. People say satya means 'be

61

truthful', yet do you know the meaning of being truthful? The real meaning of being truthful is that you are naked in front of yourself. You do not put on a different type of mask for each situation and circumstance; instead you are your natural self. The more you are your natural self, the more you adhere to the principles of satya, since you reflect what you truly are and not what you expect or project yourself to be.

Satya is also fine-tuning the mind. Satya develops an attitude of the mind that allows you to see the unreal in the environment and the untruth in your surroundings. A person who lives satya is able to know and recognize the nature of other people; to know if another person is a hypocrite or a sincere person. The person who lives satya does not hide behind an imposed identity or mask, and can therefore know the nature of other people.

It is hypocritical to talk of Ishwara pranidhana and to not talk of shaucha or santosha, which are the basic foundations for accepting life and experiencing peace in life. Patanjali said spirituality does not begin with *Ishwara pranidhana*, belief in God; no type of religious, spiritual or psychic experience begins with God. The first step is reorganizing, purifying and balancing the mind. *Shaucha*, cleanliness, is the first of the niyamas. Perfect that and pass the first class. Shaucha, the cleanliness and the purity of mind is reflected in how you live and how you think and act.

Your bedroom is a reflection of your mental state. Your closet is a reflection of your mental state. Your house is a reflection of you, whether you live your life in a disorderly manner or in an orderly manner, in a systematic manner or in an unsystematic manner. The *shuchi*, the purity, that you experience inside reflects outside in the environment as well. If you want to see the shuchi or the state of a sannyasin's or sadhaka's mind, go and see how their room and closet is. If you want to see the state of your mind, go and see your room. This is a simple, undeniable fact.

The second niyama is *santosha* or contentment. As long as there is discontentment in life, can there be any type of spiritual awareness? No. Spiritual awareness does not begin with discontentment, as discontentment is more external and not internal, mental. Discontentment relates to the senses, mind, needs, expectations, desires and ambitions; 99.9 percent of discontentment is in relation to the world, society, the family, and your own self. How can you realize your pure nature in a fractured personality?

Therefore, the basic precept that Ishwara pranidhana is yoga is inaccurate. The simple idea is that organization and purity are the beginning of your journey of discovery. The simple idea is that cultivating contentment in life is the beginning of your journey. This aspect, the second experience of yoga, enables you to make yourself a better person by realizing your traits and behaviours. Once you have attained that level of realization, and are able to modify certain traits within yourself and experience enhanced awareness and clarity, then you move into the third experience of yoga.

Third stage of practice: force of grace
The third aspect can be associated with kriya yoga. This third experience of yoga is psychic and spiritual. At this point you begin to work with kundalini, with chakras, with the energies that surround you, and you begin to work with those inherent abilities within you that are presently dormant.

When you reach the third level, you become the channel for grace, whatever shape that grace takes. Grace can take the shape of love, so you become the channel of love. Grace can take the shape of peace; you become the channel of peace, you radiate peace. Grace can become the channel of bliss; you radiate bliss.

When you begin to experience this spiritual force known in religious terminology as 'grace', then there is a sense of completeness, wholeness, and a sense of connectedness. You feel that your heart is connected with something much more powerful than what you can identify with your senses. That is the third experience of yoga.

From inspired to inspirer

The Sivananda and the Satyananda Yoga traditions focus on the second and the third stages of yoga practice, as most of the people who come here to the Bihar School of Yoga have had exposure to the physical hatha yoga stage, whether in a large quantity or a small quantity. Using that experience you then move into the second stage of yoga. Those who are able to fulfil the process of the second become inspirations to our human society. Those who complete the process of the third become an inspiration to human civilization.

7

The Wheel of
Satyananda Yoga–Bihar Yoga

The yogic theory is that if you are able to regulate all the aspects of your body, including the physical, the pranic, the mental, the consciousness, and the psychic dimensions, then any condition can be effectively managed. Even in the case of disease or a life-threatening illness, whether it is physiological, psychological or psychic, the yogic theory is that if you are able to harmonize all these five levels of your existence, you may regain balance and maintain your health.

Stress, anxiety, imbalance in the mucus-bile-wind system, obsession and hypertension are all indications of imbalances and disturbances in one's system. They are indications of different states that one goes through in one's life. When there is anxiety or worry, what tools can be used to overcome that particular expression of one's nature in the shortest time and simplest manner?

Yoga capsules for health
The system of Satyananda Yoga–Bihar Yoga covers all aspects, even for the management of stress: asana deals with the muscular and nervous stress; pranayama deals with nervous stress; yoga nidra deals with mental stress; mantra deals with the unconscious stressors; and meditation creates a bridge between your mind and the experience of peace while living in an environment of stressors. These practices of asana, pranayama, pratyahara, yoga nidra, relaxation,

concentration and mantra put together create one capsule of yoga. The minimum from all of these different aspects becomes one yoga capsule.

In order to get relief from a headache, you need only have one tablet, by which your headache will go away in ten minutes. By swallowing ten tablets, your headache will not go away in one minute. It will still take ten minutes, however, consuming ten tablets is damaging to your health. Instead, it is better to take one and have the same benefit, and similarly with yoga practice. Doing twenty practices creates more stress in your body and mind system, and will have the opposite result; while you are expecting something to happen, you will undergo a different experience. The yoga capsule deals with the minimum that you can apply in one situation and the shortest time period that you can do it in. If you can do the whole routine in fifteen minutes, that is a capsule; and the appropriate one. If you are able to sustain it you will create a conditioning whereby, in the future, stress will have no effect.

I live surrounded by stress; I do not live in spiritual bliss! I do not live in inner peace. I live surrounded by perpetual clouds of the stress, anxiety and phobias of everybody around me. Even when I go out, I am surrounded by the expectations of people and what each one desires of me. Even within the ashram, the expectations of everyone surround me. I am never free from these stressors. I do not live in spiritual bliss, samadhi and ananda; they are a distant reality in my life. Despite that, with yoga I have the skill to manage the stressors so I can be smiling all the time. While others are frowning during the day, I am smiling. That is a skill and an ability that is developed where the stressors do not affect; a positive conditioning, nature and habit are created.

Yoga capsules therefore are an important aspect of yoga, as they help to create a positive condition by eradicating that which frequently affects the peaceful state of the body and mind. That is the reason for the yoga capsules. All the different practices that you learn in your classes – asana, pranayama, concentration and meditation techniques of self-help, and the different ways to observe yourself – are put together in the capsules.

Disconnection from your own self

Since the time of birth, you are conditioned to look outwards and to keep yourself entertained. Entertainment, pleasure and enjoyment become the main focus in life. When these become the focus of life and they lead you towards sensorial gratification, then being in touch with yourself is lost. For everything you are dependent on healers, doctors, therapies and medicines. If you have a headache, you will take medicine, yet you will not change your environment, your routine, your lifestyle or your mindset. If you have anxiety you will take tablets and visit a psychologist or a psychoanalyst, and not learn how to relax the stresses and the stressors. This is the situation in which you live, and it is going to increase in the future.

The dependency on outer agents to find happiness and health will increase in the future. That is the meaning of the word 'materialism'. Everyone is attracted by it and there is not a single soul upon this planet who can say, "I am free from my attractions to and the hypnosis of materialism." After trekking many days, one traveller reached the Himalayan mountains and at twenty-one thousand feet saw a cave, inside which there was a yogi meditating. He approached the yogi, bowed down and said, "Master, please tell me the purpose of life." The yogi said, "Hold on for five minutes, I'll go and check Google and give you the answer." Even in the high mountain caves there are computers and Wi-Fi connection!

Many people know their computer more than their own body and can sort the problems of their computer when it arises. They cannot, however, sort the problems of their own body in which they live all their life. That is how disconnected they are from themselves. Some yoga students are not even aware that they have armpits or where the armpit is located! That is how disconnected people have become from their own body.

There is a disconnection from the body and mind in everyone's life. My guru, Sri Swami Satyananda, says that our actions are not compatible with our wisdom. Actions are guided by greed and need, passions and ambitions, and not by wisdom or understanding. You desire understanding and sympathy, yet you are not able to express it in your own life. This is the real encounter in the spiritual journey with yourself. Asana and pranayama reflect only a little component of this yogic journey.

In order to understand the breadth and depth of yoga, to have a glimpse of the 'yoga chakra', the wheel of yoga illustrates the different aspects of the Bihar Yoga system.

THE EARLY PERIOD	
Shiva	*Pashupata Yoga*
	1. Mantra yoga
	2. Sparsha yoga
	3. Bhava yoga
	4. Abhava yoga
	5. Maha yoga
Matsyendra Nath	*The Nath Tradition*
	1. Hatha yoga
	2. Raja yoga
	3. Kriya/Kundalini yoga
Sage Dattatreya	*Dattatreya Prokta Yogashastra*
	1. Mantra yoga
	2. Laya yoga
	3. Hatha yoga
	4. Raja yoga
Purpose:	Removal of pain and suffering in life. Attaining peace, following dharma, acting creatively.

Early, ancient wave of yoga

Before understanding the wheel of yoga, however, we start with the early period to refresh the memory. The early period of yoga starts with Shiva, the propagator of the Pashupata yoga system. In the Pashupata yoga system, five yogas are defined, which constitute the original yoga: sparsha yoga, mantra yoga, bhava yoga, abhava yoga, and maha yoga. In that period Nath yogis brought the teachings of

Sage Dattatreya

Pashupata yoga and developed them as hatha yoga, raja yoga, kriya yoga, and kundalini yoga.

The aim of yoga in the early period was never God-realization. When Shiva expounded the theory of yoga and of tantra, the purpose was to remove pain and suffering, whether self-generated, destined or environmental; transcend the pain; attain peace from the distractions and diversions of the senses and mind; follow dharma, the obligations, responsibilities, commitments and duties in the right manner; and act creatively to fulfil the aim of human destiny, which is *poornata*, wholeness and perfection .

Second, middle wave of yoga

The earlier period formed the schools of yoga, and then in the middle period the practitioners of yoga wrote their theses on particular aspects of yoga. The originators of the hatha yoga system that you follow today are Gheranda and Swatmarama. Raja yoga is Patanjali. Bhakti yoga is Shandiliya and Narada. Similarly, there are other yogas described specifically in the twenty-two yoga upanishads; such as *Yoga Chudamani Upanishad*, which is devoted to kundalini yoga and speaks of chakras and kundalini. Similarly, there are dissertations by different sages and

THE MIDDLE PERIOD

Hatha yoga	Sage Gheranda
	Yogi Swatmarama
Raja yoga	Sage Patanjali
Bhakti yoga	Sage Shandilya
	Sage Narada
Other yogas	22 yoga upanishads
	Other sages, e.g. Sage Vasishtha, etc.
Purpose:	Regulating lifestyle, discovering the self, living righteously.

practitioners of yoga in twenty-one other Upanishads on the different yogas.

By looking at their writings and their teachings you can see that the purpose of yoga at that time was regulating the lifestyle. That emphasis is predominantly visible in the upanishadic tradition of yoga. The premise is that your lifestyle, how you live, your routine and your environment, determines how far you can advance in the experience of yoga. The purpose of yoga was to discover one's self, to discover the self that interacts at the outer material level in the world of senses and sense objects, and the self that exists beyond the fetters of the senses, sense objects and mind; and with this realization, to live righteously. That was the second generation of the middle period of yoga.

Third, contemporary wave of yoga

There have been many yoga propagators in the present period. Yogi Rama Charaka and Swami Vivekananda presented the theory of the four yogas: raja yoga, karma yoga, jnana yoga, and bhakti yoga. Then emerged the tradition of Babaji, Lahiri Mahashaya, Sri Yukteshwar Giri and Paramahamsa Yogananda. Paramahamsa Yogananda brought forth the teaching of kriya yoga. A contemporary around that time was Swami Sivananda, who taught integral yoga to his disciples. His disciples became the first-generation teachers and the propagators of yoga in the world.

Swami Sivananda and Anandamayi Ma

Sri B.K.S. Iyengar brought to the forefront the concept of the South Indian hatha yoga for connecting with the body. Similarly, Ramana Maharshi propagated the concept of jnana yoga, the self-discovery by questioning yourself, 'Who am I?' Bhaktivedanta Swami Prabhupada propagated an aspect of bhakti yoga. Anandamayi Ma

---

THE PRESENT/RECENT PERIOD

Yogi Ram Charak	Theory of yoga
Swami Vivekananda	Theory of yoga
Paramahamsa Yogananda	Kriya yoga
Swami Sivananda (and his disciples)	Integral yoga
Sri B.K.S. Iyenger	Hatha yoga
Ramana Maharshi	Jnana yoga
Bhaktivedanta Swami Praphupad	Bhakti
Anandamayi Ma	Bhakti
Other Unnamed Yogis	Use yoga as personal sadhana

Purpose: Uniting head, heart and hands. Discovering the creative self, attaining samadhi as integral expression of the awakened self.

propagated bhakti. Swami Chinmayananda propagated jnana yoga. Baba Muktananda propagated mantra yoga.

Apart from these mainstream propagators, there are still many other practitioners of yoga who live yoga, practising in isolation in the mountains or away from social interaction. Sometimes people visit them and learn a particular aspect of yoga from them, however, it does not belong to the mainstream of yoga; it is the particular sadhana of a person who is living that lifestyle in isolation. These are the unnamed yogis who use yoga as a personal sadhana. Sometimes they teach to one, two or three people, who then go out and teach that, yet it is not in the mainstream of yoga.

The purpose of yoga in the contemporary age is, again, not emancipation. The purpose of the present-day yoga is uniting the faculties of head, heart and hands, the 'triple H'. By uniting these faculties you discover the creative self; and by discovering the creative self, attain samadhi. Samadhi here is not Patanjali's definition of samadhi; it is Swami Niranjan's definition of samadhi: the integral expression of your awakened self. *Sama* means equal, harmonious, balanced; and *dhi* is intelligence. Thus *samadhi* is not the state of illumination; it is a state where you attain balance in your intelligence. You do not steer to the right or to the left; you tread the middle path. That is the state of samadhi. This is also a statement by Sri Krishna in the *Bhagavad Gita* when he was asked, "How do you define a person who has attained the state of samadhi?" Krishna says, "That person is equipoised in intellect, *sthita prajna*. One who is equipoised, balanced and harmonious in intelligence attains samadhi." That is following the middle path.

The wheel of Satyananda Yoga–Bihar Yoga

The Government of India recognizes four yoga institutions in the country: the Bihar School of Yoga, Sivananda Ashram, Vivekananda Kendra, and Kaivalyadhama.

The classical systems in Bihar Yoga are hatha yoga, raja yoga and kriya yoga as identified and taught by our guru, Sri Swami Satyananda. The sub-yogas which complement the attainments of hatha yoga, raja yoga and kriya yoga, are karma yoga, jnana yoga and bhakti yoga. They are also supported by other yogas such as mantra yoga, nada yoga, laya yoga and kundalini yoga, along with yajnas, which regulate lifestyle and connect you with the cosmic forces that surround you.

	TODAY	
Recognized Yoga Institutions	1. Bihar School of Yoga 2. Sivananda Ashram 3. Vivekananda Kendra 4. Kaivalyadhama	
	CLASSICAL YOGA IN THE BSY TRADITION	
Main	Hatha yoga Raja yoga Kriya yoga	
Sub-yogas	Karma yoga Jnana yoga Bhakti yoga	
Sub-sub yogas	Mantra yoga Nada yoga Kundalini yoga Laya yoga	
Yajnas	Shakti, Shiva, Narayana, Lakshmi, other classical yajnas	

PERFECTING INNER EXPERIENCE
THROUGH ANTARANGA YOGA

HATHA YOGA
1. Shatkarma
2. Asana*
3. Pranayama
4. Mudra
5. Bandha

RAJA YOGA
1. Yama
2. Niyama
3. Asana
4. Pranayama
5. Pratyahara
6. Dharana
7. Dhyana
8. Samadhi

KRIYA YOGA
1. Pratyahara
2. Dharana
3. Dhyana

*Viral

These create the complete system of yoga. This system is divided into antaranga yoga for self-perfection and bahiranga yoga to express the spiritual attainment.

PERFECTING INNER EXPERIENCE THROUGH ANTARANGA YOGA

I. Hatha yoga (5 stages)

Traditionally, classical hatha yoga has five aspects: shat-karma, asana, pranayama, mudra, and bandha. Asanas are the only aspect of hatha yoga that have gone viral. The ironic part is that the yoga teachers largely profess to teach in the name of Patanjali, however, they give the teachings of Swatmarama. They confuse Patanjali's teachings with hatha yoga asanas, which creates a false awareness or identity of yoga, since Patanjali has nothing to do with the asanas that have gone viral.

II. Raja yoga (8 stages)

In the raja yoga system there are eight *angas* or limbs: yama, niyama, asana, pranayama, pratyahara, dharana, dhyana, and samadhi.

III. Kriya yoga (3 stages)

In the kriya yoga system, Swami Satyananda's system is the open one. Openly he started the teaching of kriya yoga by a postal sadhana course lasting three years.

The Satyananda Yoga system of kriya yoga is divided into three categories: pratyahara kriyas, dharana kriyas, and dhyana kriyas. Although the practices combine techniques of asana, pranayama, mudras, bandhas, visualization and awareness, their focus is on perfecting, developing and deepening the state of pratyahara, dharana and dhyana. With this, a different experience of the self emerges.

KARMA YOGA
1. Atmashuddhi
2. Akarta bhava
3. Naishkarma
   Siddhi

JNANA YOGA
1. Shubheksha
2. Vicharana
3. Tanumansa
4. Sattwapatti
5. Asamsakti
6. Padartha Bhavana
7. Turyaga

BHAKTI YOGA
1. Apara Bhakti
(Karma Kanda*/
Upasana Kanda)
2. Para Bhakti
(Jnana Kanda)

*Karma kanda linked to
religious belief – Viral

EXPRESSING THE ATTAINMENT THROUGH BAHIRANGA YOGA

Expressing the attainment in your action, behaviour and thought is known as *bahiranga yoga*, or the expressive yoga. To create the complete system of yoga, this is the other half of the pie that not even the sannyasins and residents of the ashram know about, yet they live it every day.

I. Karma yoga (3 stages)

Bahiranga yoga begins with karma yoga, since nobody can be without karma. Karma is the main foundation and stay of life. The classical definition of karma yoga is that it leads you to immunity to karmas. One can define karma yoga in many ways, however, what is the purpose according to the yogis and the yogic scriptures? The purpose is not something conjured up by your intellect.

The first aspect of karma yoga is atmashuddhi: *Yoginah karma kurvanti sangam tyaktvatmashuddhaye* – "Yogis perform karma, with objectivity, for self-purification." That is the first philosophy of karma yoga. This *atmashuddhi* or self-purification contains an important word: objectivity. You have to understand objectivity not from the perspective of attachment or detachment, but simply as knowing. When you know then you manage the responses of either attachment or detachment in a better manner. Whether you are attached or detached does not matter. Therefore awareness of objectivity, in relation to your actions, leads to self-awareness, harmony, inner balance, or purification. Attainment of this leads to akarta bhava. *Karta* is the idea of doership, 'I am the doer', while *akarta* is not having the idea of doership, 'I am not the doer'. The third aspect of karma yoga is *naishkarma siddhi*, freedom from action, which is the attainment of karma yoga.

II. Jnana yoga (7 stages)

Jnana yoga has seven aspects or seven stages of progress. Jnana yoga is not discovery of self by questioning and answering yourself, 'Who am I? I am the Eternal Spirit', and then forgetting that you are the Eternal Spirit and instead becoming the eternal enjoyer in life. That is not jnana yoga. Jnana yoga does not, as written everywhere, begin with a question; it begins with *shubheksha*, the right intention for yourself; the right understanding arising out of the correct awareness, creating a right desire and intention within yourself to discover who you are. That is the first step and it leads to gradual 'subtlization' of the mind; the mind becomes more and more subtle in each stage as you progress into vicharana, tanumansa, sattwapati, asamsakti, padarthabhava and turiyaga. In the turiyaga state of jnana you simply identify with the bliss or *ananda* that comes out of understanding and out of knowing. When ananda comes from knowing then your actions, behaviour, and everything in you are a reflection of the luminosity of your wisdom.

III. Bhakti yoga (9 stages)

The third aspect of bahiranga yoga is bhakti yoga, which people only think of in relation to kirtans, bhajans, worships, rituals and images. There are nine stages of bhakti, however, the nine stages are divided in two categories: para bhakti and apara bhakti, the transcendental and the non-transcendental. The *para*, the transcendental, in the domain of yoga is the jnana kanda of bhakti. *Apara* is in the domain of regular people, the householders and the sadhakas who are living in the world, and relates to the karma kanda and upasana kanda aspect. The whole purpose of this is to create a connection, a bridge, between your lower self and your higher self.

SUMMARY

When you put the two halves of the chakra together, then the understanding of the yoga that we practise in the Satyananda Yoga–Bihar Yoga tradition becomes complete. That is the wheel of yoga.

SATYANANDA YOGA–BIHAR YOGA CHAKRA

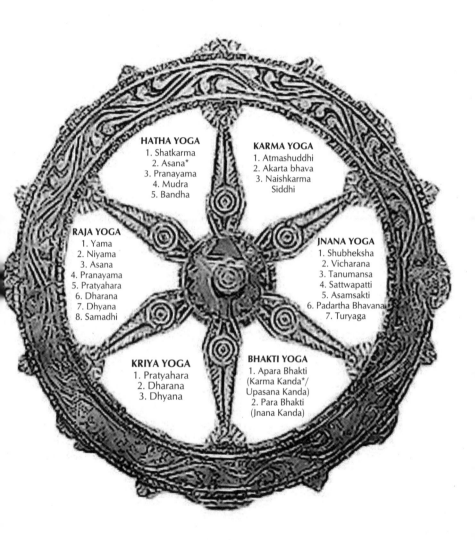

HATHA YOGA
1. Shatkarma
2. Asana*
3. Pranayama
4. Mudra
5. Bandha

KARMA YOGA
1. Atmashuddhi
2. Akarta bhava
3. Naishkarma
   Siddhi

RAJA YOGA
1. Yama
2. Niyama
3. Asana
4. Pranayama
5. Pratyahara
6. Dharana
7. Dhyana
8. Samadhi

JNANA YOGA
1. Shubheksha
2. Vicharana
3. Tanumansa
4. Sattwapatti
5. Asamsakti
6. Padartha Bhavana
7. Turyaga

KRIYA YOGA
1. Pratyahara
2. Dharana
3. Dhyana

BHAKTI YOGA
1. Apara Bhakti
(Karma Kanda*/
Upasana Kanda)
2. Para Bhakti
(Jnana Kanda)

Notes